The writer of the book of Lamentations, whose word title of this book, speaks of times – often hard and (– when the Word and Spirit of God come to us in n inspire and challenge us to move forward (3.22). A amazing characteristic of this Prayer Handbook.

Morning

Each year, the freshness of prayers and insights from people whose experience of life is so diverse makes it an enriching and challenging tool for prayer. This year, you will find exciting glimpses of the Spirit at work: churches in Britain and Ireland whose life and worship have been enriched by the coming of asylum seekers and by newcomers brought in through Alpha courses, ecumenical initiatives at all levels, people whose livelihood was swept away by flood, or devastated by earthquake or warfare... finding strength to begin again. That too was the experience of the writer of Lamentations.

- As you pray, know that you are praying *with* those who have written the prayers.
- Don't worry if you do not have time to use all the material for each day. Select and focus on different aspects and places each month.
- If you do not know what all the symbols mean, see the key on page 80.
- Use your newspaper and make sure that the concerns of each new day are remembered.
- Add your own prayers. Use the spaces in the margins to include the names of people you know who need your support.
- Use the Lectionary readings on pages 74-79. These link with the Bible reading notes of the International Bible Reading Association (see page 80).

New every year

This book, which is compiled afresh every year, contains prayers for each day of each month and ensures that all the Churches with which we have a partnership and each of the Districts in Britain and Ireland (see page 61) are remembered. Those of you who are familiar with it will notice some changes: this is mainly to provide extra space for prayers for partner Churches in Latin America and Europe with whom we have developed a closer relationship over the last 15-20 years.

Maureen Edwards

Prayer Handbook Committee
Maureen Edwards
(Editor)
Susan Johnson
Michael King
Norman Wallwork
Sarah Middleton
Brian Thornton
Robert S Russell

Cover design
Robyn Timm

Layout
Audrey Facey

An outline for Morning and Evening Prayer

Open our lips, O Lord,
And we shall praise your name.
Glory to the Father, and to the Son,
and to the Holy Spirit:
As it was in the beginning, is now,
and shall be for ever. Amen
*(From Easter to Pentecost: **Alleluia**)*

Hymn *

Psalm * and *Glory to the Father*

Scripture *

Canticle from *Hymns and Psalms*

Morning	Evening
S 825	S 826
M 833	M 828
T 824	T 831
W 832	W 829
T 831	T 830
F 829	F 644
S 830	S 832

The Lord's Prayer

Collect of the Day or of the Week

Morning Collect
Lord our God, as with all creation, we offer you the life of this new day; give us grace to love and serve you to the praise of Jesus Christ our Lord. **Amen**

Evening Collect
Lord our God, at the ending of this day, and in the darkness and silence of this night, cover us with healing and forgiveness, that we may take our rest in peace, through Jesus Christ our Lord.
Amen

Thanksgiving

Intercession

The Grace

* See Lectionary pp74-79

An outline for a Preaching Service

Welcome and Call to Worship

Hymn

Prayers:
   Invocation or Adoration
   Confession
   Declaration of Forgiveness
   Collect of the Day

Hymn

Old Testament Lesson

Psalm

Lesson from the Apostles (Epistle)

Hymn

Lesson from the Gospels

Sermon

Hymn

Prayers
   Thanksgiving (for Creation, Redemption in Christ and the life of the Church in the Spirit);
   Intercession * (for the Church and its mission; for the world and its communities; for the sick and those in need; specific petitions and remembrance of those who have died).

   The Lord's Prayer

Notices

Offering and Prayer at the Offering

Hymn

Blessing and Dismissal

* *Including relevant day in Prayer Handbook*

New Every Morning

For personal devotion or public worship

Presence

Lord of the morning,
in my sleeping and in my waking
I am blessed by your love.
Help me, this day, to be so alive
to the constancy of your care
that my thoughts and actions might reflect
your presence;
that I might be attentive in listening,
kind in speaking,
patient with mistakes,
generous in encouragement
and so open to laughter
that this day might be remembered
for the joy that the knowledge
of your nearness brings. Amen

Frank Topping, Barnet

Thanksgiving

New every morning
the sun rises, we say.
But it was always shining;
rather, we turned to face it.
So, constant, shining God,
may we turn heart and mind to you
and find new light and life.

New every morning
the waking world
takes colour,
starts its sounds again,
begins to move –
your creatures, Lord,
responding to your light.
So, renewing God,
may we awake to you.

But Lord,
where street lights blot out stars,
where traffic is unceasing,
cities never stop
and shops never close,
there, dawn means little.
Still in your mercy,
never-sleeping God,
shine your eternal light
and wake us up to you.

New every morning
the world's promise and its need:
children to feed and teach,
livings to earn and homes to build,
discoveries to make, dangers to avoid,
damage to make good,
injustices to fight...
So much to do, Lord.

New every morning
the energy for loving –
the Spirit of Christ crucified
(whom death could not hold),
poured from the Father's heart,
at large among us;
empowering all
who would be cross-bearers
in their turn,
partners in his unceasing work.
Lord, may we be among them,
relying on your grace,
longing for your Kingdom,
and trusting it to come.

New every morning...
depths of God to explore,
wonders of God to praise,
words of God to hear,
presence of God to realise,
promises of God to claim,
love of God to live by:
Let us bless the Lord,
Thanks be to God.

*Christina Le Moignan,
President of the Methodist Conference*

Confession

It is not a tall spire or steeple bell that
calls us to worship
but a stark cross against a silent sky:
Lord have mercy.
There is no aisle or majestic vaulting
leading to your altar
but a pathway of pain and insults – denial
by friends:
Christ have mercy.
It is not the costly vestments
that draw the eye
or the sombre liturgy that stirs
the heart
but a naked man
with outstretched arms
surpassing, surrounding, inhabiting
our separation and suffering:
Lord have mercy.
No flowers here or fragrant incense
but a crown of thorns and the deep red of
self-giving love:
Christ have mercy.
Where are your friends
to greet you and thank you
for the work you have done?
There are none,
only the separation caused by sin
felt fully in the heart of God:
Lord have mercy, Christ have mercy.
Janet Corlett, Forest circuit, London

Intercession

God of eternity,
as the crowds welcomed Jesus
and sang your praises,
we ourselves welcome you
and we pray that many more
will welcome you this year.
We pray for strength and courage
to live out your Word,
bringing justice, peace and hope
to the world *(silence)*.

We pray for the Church:
may we find a way of being 'church'
that will answer the needs
of our communities...
a way that will reach out
to those who feel too busy
to come to church
or who find us too regulated,
and yet who serve you
in many different ways.
Give us your wisdom,
that we may find a way
to nurture each other in faith
and build each other up in love *(silence)*.

God of love,
as the crowds responded
to the healing love they saw in Jesus,
in prayer we bring to you
those who need your healing
and encouraging love.
We think of… … …
giving thanks for the skill and care
of medical staff *(silence)*.

God of grace,
may we find a way
to live side by side,
embracing our diversity.
May we find a way to bring healing
and peace to our fractured world.
We think of… … … *(silence)*

God of wisdom,
as Jesus knew that he was riding
into Jerusalem to his death,
we too know that we must one day
make that journey.
As we hold the cup of life
in our hands,
we pray for a deeper understanding
of your Word and courage,
that we may live each day to the full,

thanking you for both our sorrows
and our joys,
as we follow our own unique journeys.

We commend to your eternal love
all who have already made that journey
and those who grieve today *(silence)*.
As we listen each day,
may we hear your voice,
the voice that calls us 'Beloved'.
We pray in Jesus' name. Amen

Elizabeth Hopner,
Aotearoa/New Zealand

For the unloved

God, Father and Mother of us all,
You brought the universe into being.
You brought us into being.
In your sight we are all equal.
Each of us is loved unconditionally
  by you.

You place us in relationships
  with one another.
You place us in relationships
  within families.
You place us in relationships
  with friends.
You place us in relationships
  across the world.

All of us are sisters and brothers
  in your family.
All of us are sisters and brothers
  in your love.

We pray for those who feel unloved.
We pray for those who cannot love
  themselves.
We pray for those who cannot accept
  your love.

Ann Leck, Vice-President
of the Methodist Conference

For today

God of the morning,
help us to live this day to the full.
We rejoice in the sun rising,
blessing each blade of grass,
dwelling on the detail of creation,
rock and tree and living creature,
light dancing on the waves.
We rejoice in dawn
opening up city streets,
nightly locked in fear and loneliness.
We catch the rhythm
as the wheels of the world
begin to turn:
workers on their way,
schoolchildren skipping,
shops opening, neighbours meeting.
May we be open
to this day's uniqueness,
receive all that it offers,
and use it for good.
May we not worry about the future
any more than the birds of the air.
May we live this day
as though it is our last,
and by living it to the full
glorify you here and now. Amen

Jan S Pickard, Iona Community

Blessing

May Christ of the gentle mists
hide you.
May Christ of the falling rain
refresh you.
May Christ of the scudding clouds
o'ershadow you.
May Christ of the rising sun
illumine you.
May Christ of the winding way
draw you safe home. Amen

Stephen Caddy, Isle of Man

Africa

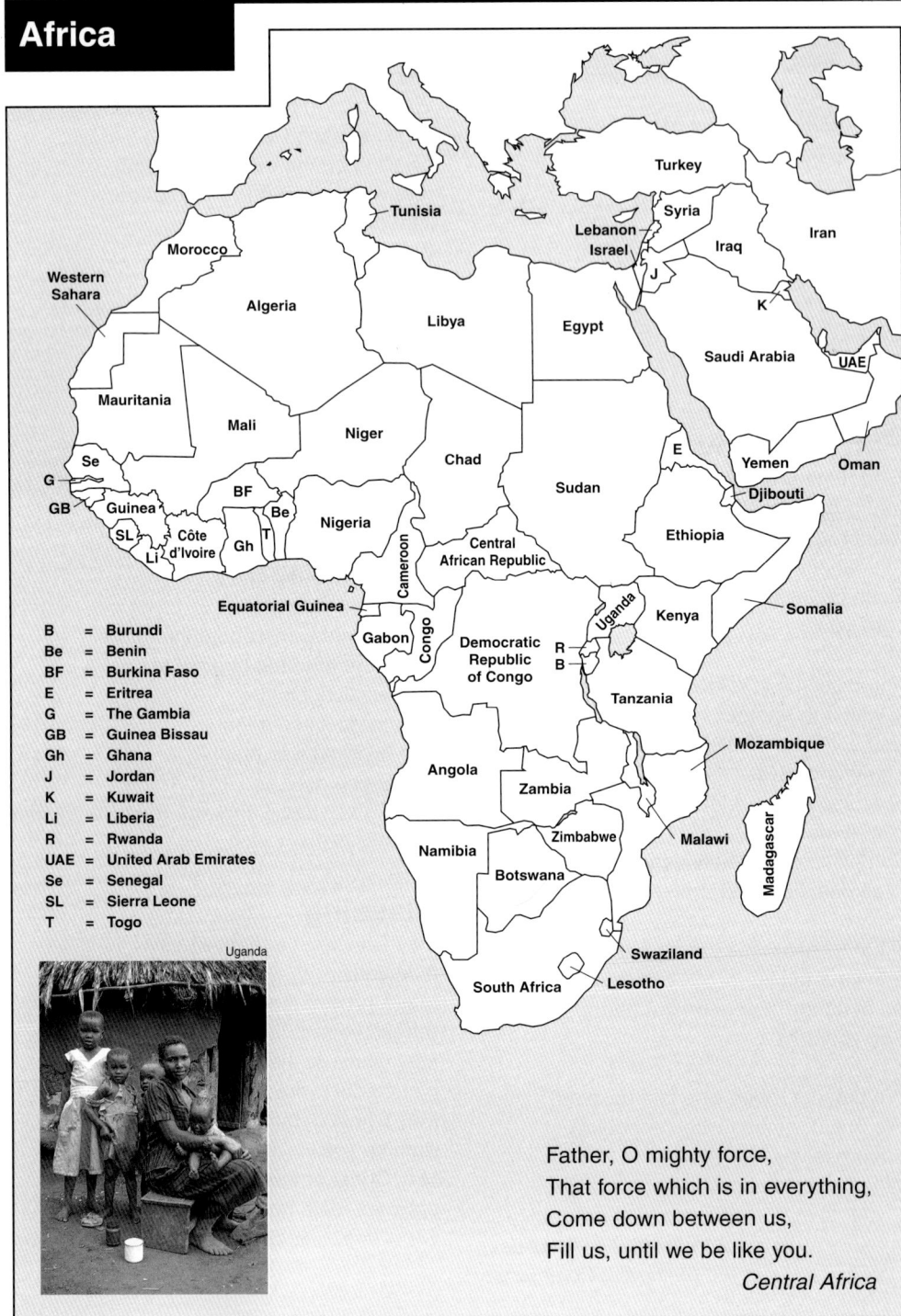

B = Burundi
Be = Benin
BF = Burkina Faso
E = Eritrea
G = The Gambia
GB = Guinea Bissau
Gh = Ghana
J = Jordan
K = Kuwait
Li = Liberia
R = Rwanda
UAE = United Arab Emirates
Se = Senegal
SL = Sierra Leone
T = Togo

Father, O mighty force,
That force which is in everything,
Come down between us,
Fill us, until we be like you.
Central Africa

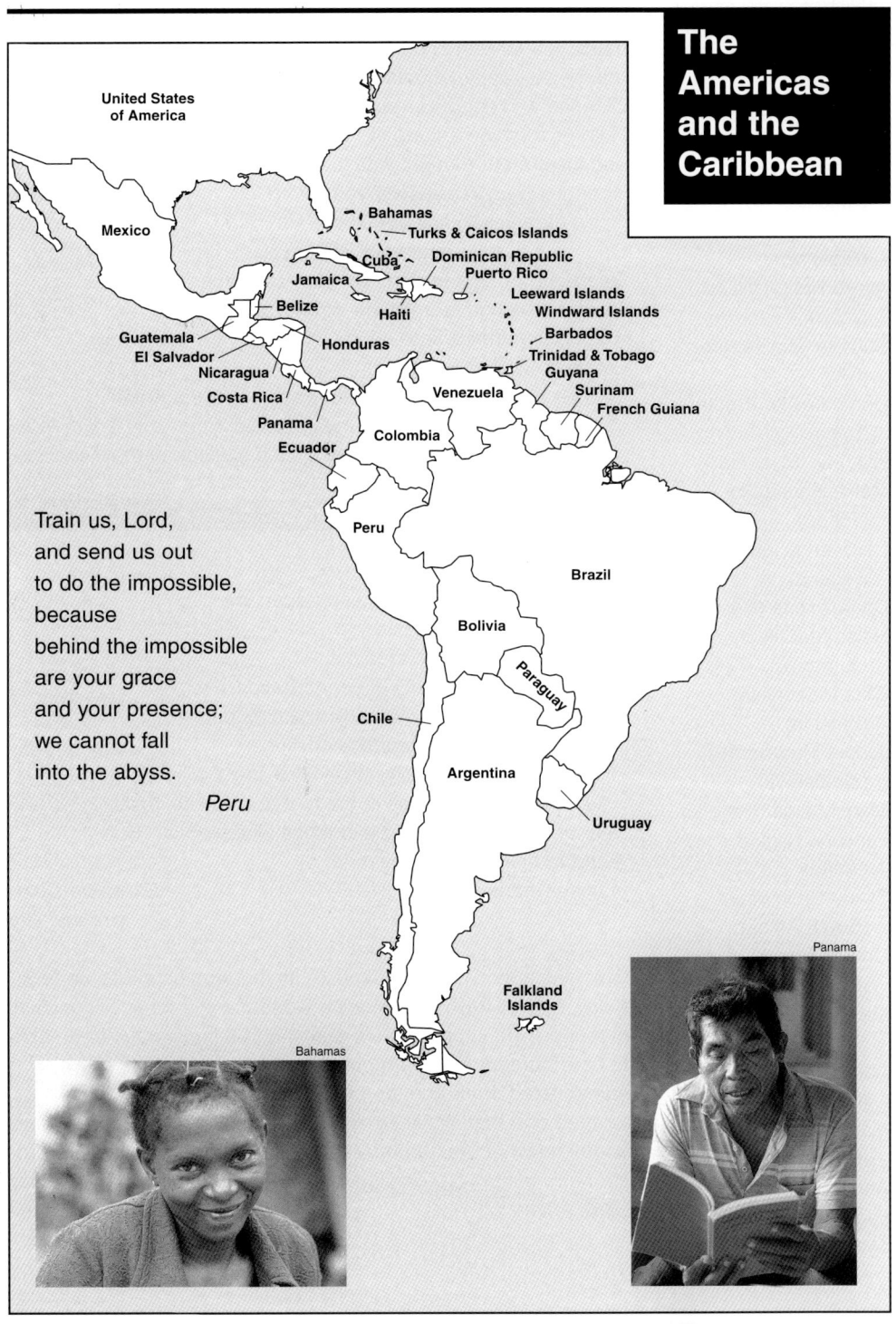

The Americas and the Caribbean

Train us, Lord,
and send us out
to do the impossible,
because
behind the impossible
are your grace
and your presence;
we cannot fall
into the abyss.

Peru

DAY 1

Scholarship students studying in Britain:
Joshua Adeogun° (Nigeria)
Oladapo Babalola° (Nigeria)
Ayoko Bahun-Wilson (Togo)
Subrata Chakrabarty° (CNI)
Deryn Fowler (South Africa)
Htay Kyi (Myanmar)
Maika Haupeakui (Tonga)
Chikwendu Igwe° (Nigeria)
Daria Yudina (Russia)
Helen Mallalieu° (Jamaica)
Elika Mbambala° (Zambia)
Jannet Mudavanhu° (Zimbabwe)
Mary Mutiga° (Kenya)
Lansana Njigba° (Sierra Leone)
Sijadu Nkomonde° (South Africa)
Charity Nwe Lin Tin (Myanmar)
Michaiah Olaniyi (Nigeria)
Abedu Quashie (Ghana)
Maylin Richards (Belize)
Anna Seregina (Russia)
Faga Semesi (Fiji)
Sydney Sichilima (Zambia)

God of the ages and our parents,
thank you for rest and the freshness of morning:
before we see any human face, you show us your glory.
Cleanse and keep us from all evil this day.
Help us to shine among the poor as the morning sun,
and inspire our thought with love like the sun at noon.
Strengthen us to translate your Word into deeds.
Open our eyes to see you in the natural world;
Open our ears to hear your loving voice;
Open our mouths to proclaim your salvation;
Open our hands to uplift the downtrodden;
And open our hearts to be in fellowship with you always.
Let us so walk in your light
that the glory and honour will always be yours. Amen
*D Soundararadan, Church of South India,
student at the United College of the Ascension*

Praying with the whole creation

Creator God
You looked upon the world you had made
   and pronounced it good.
Help us to work as co-creators,
   to protect the integrity of your creation.
We pray for farmers who battle the elements
   and the markets to produce our food.
We remember especially, those who saw their life's work
   turn to dust and ashes in the foot-and-mouth crisis.
Help us to value the land and those who work it,
   and to ensure a fair share for all.
In Jesus' name. Amen
Elizabeth Clark, York and Hull

Gracious and ever-loving God, in all the problems that we face today, both in town and country, we thank you for your constant presence and support. We thank you that many have been able to bear burdens and surmount disappointments in a way that has amazed them and the people around them. We thank you for the hope that is still within us, and for the confidence to face an unknown future. We offer this prayer, not trusting in our own strength, but in your changeless love, through Jesus Christ, our Lord. Amen
The Arthur Rank Centre

Praying with Christians in Britain

'The Lord's love is surely not exhausted,
nor has his compassion failed:
they are new every morning' *(Lamentations 3.22 REB).*
These words from the 6th century BC spoke of hope when the tragic destruction of Jerusalem threatened the identity of a whole people.
Along with all our ecumenical partners, we live in a rapidly changing world. Reflect on the challenges of
- being a multi-faith, multi-cultural society,
- more diverse and less stable patterns of family life,
- different forms of spirituality,
- sharp divisions between rural and urban society,
- large scale movements of people across many parts of the world.

Pray for every part of the Methodist Church as we seek to fulfil **'Our Calling'** – to respond to the gospel of God's love in Christ and to live our discipleship in worship and mission:
for an increasing awareness of God's presence and confidence in celebrating God's love;
for mutual support and care as we seek to grow and learn as Christian people;
for a faithful response to specific needs and the readiness to challenge injustice;
for commitment to calling people to faith in Jesus Christ.

Peter Sulston

President of British Methodist Conference:
Christina Le Moignan
Vice-President:
Ann Leck
Youth President:
Ellie O'Malley
Network President:
Beryl Cowling
Secretary of Conference:
Nigel Collinson
Assistant Secretary:
Keith Reed
Co-ordinating Secretaries:
David Deeks
Jonathan Kerry
Ruby Beech
Peter Sulston

Give thanks for the ministry among children and young people around the District, and for the many young people who have been confirmed and received into membership over the past year.
Pray for the District's Mission Enabling Group as it works with churches and circuits to help them respond to the vision of 'Our Calling'.

Creator God,
As we consider the works of your hands,
Help us to cherish the gift of life;
As we learn more of life's beginning,
Teach us also to be mindful of its End
And fill each day with your glory. Amen

Ermal Kirby

London North East District

Chair:
Ermal Kirby
Secretary:
Clifford Newman

Give thanks for the order and beauty of created things

DAY 2

Father, all loving and most tender, we confess the hardness of our hearts and our want of compassion for our neighbour. Grant us the grace of true pity, the ministry of compassion and the gift of consoling the broken-hearted. Teach us to love with your own forbearance and never harshly or unlovingly to judge another; for your own mercies' sake. Amen

Johann Arndt, 1555-1621

Praying with Christians in West Africa (1)

The Gambia District

Chair: Titus Pratt

Mission partners:
p Robbie Bowen°
n Ruth Bowen

Give thanks for Christian witness in a predominantly Muslim society;
for projects which serve the people and for the quality of education given in Methodist schools.
Pray for the work of the agricultural project which includes well-digging and involves over 300 farmers, two-thirds of whom are women – for increasing productivity in an environmentally sustainable way;
for the work of the Marakissa nutrition and maternity units;
for preparations being made for this last overseas District of the Methodist Church in Britain to become autonomous.

Sierra Leone

Methodist President:
Francis Nabieu

Special appointment:
Michael Moss

Give thanks for a people who face their suffering with resilience and hope;
for ministers and lay people who are closely involved in the community, identifying needs and doing all they can to address the problems.
Pray with people who have experienced nights of terror: more than once forced out of their homes which were then set alight... people who have witnessed the murder of their family and friends... people who know desolation...
for all who are involved in aiding rehabilitation and trauma counselling;
for camps of displaced people (over half the population);
for a new project to resettle ministers and catechists in their villages so that they can provide leadership and stability, and help and encourage returning refugees to rebuild their communities.

'Let us not give up; it will happen in God's own time. God still cares. See how much everyone is getting involved in Britain, America, the OAU and the UN! And the prayers of friends.'

Albert Lahai

Praying with Christians in Ireland

As Ireland, north and south, faces change our Christian faith calls us to move beyond the boundaries of our experience and be confronted by the future.

The peace process in Northern Ireland has set the framework in which we may build new relationships inside the province and beyond. The Christian community exists to build relationships with others and to reach out and embrace especially those from whom we have felt alienated. Methodists have prayed and persuaded and played their part in the process of reconciliation.

In the Republic of Ireland the 'tiger economy' has brought wealth to some, poverty to others. The country was not prepared for the sudden turn-around from emigration to immigration. The churches have been at the forefront in the welcome of refugees and asylum seekers, many of whom are enriching the worship and life of our churches. The battle against racism and greed needs to be constant as we face the challenge of a multi-faith society.

Pray for the Republic of Ireland and for a compassionate and inclusive multi-ethnic society;
for the Northern Ireland Peace Process;
for all Irish Church leaders and evangelical, ecumenical encounters.

Kenneth Todd

President of Methodist Church in Ireland:
Harold Good
Secretary of Irish Conference:
Edmund Mawhinney

Methodist Women's Association President:
Margaret Taggart

Give thanks for enrichment experienced by congregations who welcome refugees, asylum seekers and economic migrants and the opportunity to develop bi-lingual worship;
for counselling services being offered at Madley in Bray, the new hall and new opportunities in Wicklow.
Pray for the construction of the Methodist Centre in Tallaght;
for closer links with Dublin Central Mission;
for the new team initiative in the Blackrock Youth Outreach;
for the proposed music centre at Wesley College and the opportunity to contribute to education.

Lord, in times of large opportunity and fast-changing circumstances give us the big vision. May your work not be curtailed by past ways of ministry; give us clean, focused aims and the grace to leave the outcome to you. Amen

Thomas Kingston

Dublin District

Superintendent:
Thomas Kingston
Secretary:
R Donaldson Rodgers

Give thanks for the resources of the earth

DAY 3

Glory to you, O Champion of all Loves, who for our sake endured the cross, encountered the enemy and tasted death. Glory be to you, O King of all Kings, who for our salvation wrestled with principalities and powers, subdued the forces of hell and won the greatest of all victories. To you be all praise, all glory and all love; now and for ever. Amen.

Thomas Ken, 1637-1711

Praying with Christians in West Africa (2)

Togo

Methodist President:
Matthias Creppy

Rejoice and give thanks with Methodists in Togo for their new status as an autonomous Church.
Pray for the work of 'La Bonne Semence', a new training centre for women (partly funded by Network) which offers tuition in sewing, dyeing, cooking and literacy, to help to raise the status of women in both Church and society.

Benin

Methodist President:

Give thanks for those who work to bring about reconciliation in the deeply divided Methodist Church in Benin, especially those from the partner Methodist Churches of Britain, Côte d'Ivoire and Nigeria.
We pray for dialogue between the separated communities and for the healing of wounds that keep them apart;
for the continuing partnership between the Methodist Church in Britain and the Methodist Church in Benin;
for the Protestant Institute of Theology and the Polyclinic of the Good Samaritan in Porto-Novo;
for the health centre in Za-Tanta.

Côte d'Ivoire

Methodist President:
Benjamin Boni

Mission partners:
n/m Shirley and Yao Assandey N'Guessan, Stan, Geni and Rory

Give thanks for the faithful who have worked hard for reconciliation.
Pray for Church leaders who are involved in trying to solve the aftermath of conflict in our country;
for relationships with other Churches;
for Dabou Hospital and its developing obstetric unit;
for the Bacadi Maternity Clinic;
for the Christian Bookshop project in Sikensi.

Shirley N'Guessan

'God has a soft spot for sinners.
His standards are quite low.'

Archbishop Desmond Tutu

Praying with Christians in Britain and Ireland

We give thanks for increasing ecumenical co-operation in Milton Keynes and Aylesbury, and for a new covenant signed in Bedford where new housing estates are planned.
Pray for the continuing work of the West London Mission with its care for the poor;
for work among students from many parts of the world at the Methodist International Centre in Euston, at the students' hostel at Kings Cross Methodist Mission and for all our work with students through chaplaincy in London.

London North West District

Chair:
Garth Rogers
Secretary:
Brian King

Mission partners:
Bernardino and Elizabeth Mandlate (Mozambique)

Give thanks for the development of new ecumenical congregations at Elvetham Heath, Fleet and at the Haven School, Eastbourne.
Pray for the developing work at Westminster Central Hall and the refurbishment programme for the Great Hall;
for the deepening relationship with ecumenical partners and the challenges and opportunities this raises;
for circuits that face staffing shortages and for new ways of ministry to develop.

'Bind us together, Lord, bind us together
With cords that cannot be broken.'
'Blest be the tie that binds...'
The trouble is, Lord,
I do not wish to be bound;
to feel the biting cords of prejudice,
or poverty, or power abused.
Neither, Lord, do I wish to be tied,
with rope that is indestructible,
unyielding, imprisoning,
and from which I can never break free.
Let me rather pray
'Freedom between us, Lord, freedom between us!
Where trust is stronger than bondage',
so that closeness in Christ to my neighbour
becomes a holy and reverent holding,
leaving no evidence of rope marks,
only the fingerprints of love. Amen
    Val Ogden, tutor at the United College of the Ascension

London South West District

Chair:
Martin Broadbent
Secretary:
David Chapman

Westminster Central Hall

Methodist Diaconal Order Warden:
Margaret Matta

Give thanks for the gift of human life

DAY 4

Sever us, O Lord, from our own selves and graft us into your own being. Let us perish to ourselves that we may be safe in you. Let us die to ourselves that we may live in you. Let us wither to ourselves that we may blossom in you and let us be empty to ourselves that we may flourish in you; now and forever. Amen

Desiderius Erasmus, 1466-1536

Praying with Christians in West Africa (3)

Equatorial Guinea

Methodist Lay President:
Cristino Daniel Collins

Give thanks that a large proportion of the population is Christian.
Pray for those who suffer arrest and torture, including some Roman Catholic priests, for mainly ethnic reasons.

Ghana

Presiding Bishop:
Samuel Asante-Antwi

Mission partners:
p/ed Alan° and Pam Harvey
ee   Doris Frost

Give thanks for the work of the Revd Michael Sackey (a National in Mission appointment supported by the World Church Office), planting new congregations in a spirit of holistic evangelism. We pray for continued growth and for the maturity of Christians who are formed by this programme.
Give thanks for the vitality and confidence of Ghanaian communities in Britain and their significant contribution to our society.
Pray for the Ghanaian Methodists worshipping in British congregations;
for the 50-strong Ghanaian fellowship at Westminster Central Hall as it plans to provide language classes for children and adults in Britain to promote Ghanaian culture.

Loving God, Creator of all things,
all that is and all that is yet to be,
we bow down to worship you.
Merciful Father, our ever present help in times of trouble, our hope and inspiration: reveal yourself to us now.
When we are in doubt and when we are fearful,
help us to recognise you.
When dark clouds fill our skies,
teach us to seek your wonderful way with joy and hope.
Let your light shine through our sorrows, grief and pain,
and guide us in your power to seek your love.
In Jesus' name we pray. Amen

Roberta Mettle-Nunoo, Ghana/Redhill

Praying with Christians in Britain and Ireland

Give thanks for the energy and perspective asylum seekers and refugees have brought to our churches and communities.
Pray for the renewal of worship in our churches as we seek to serve Christ in an era of shifting values;
for the new work in Kilkee and Kilrush, work among New Age settlers, and for recovery in the agricultural sector.

Midlands and Southern District (Ireland)

Superintendent:
David Range
Secretary:
John Sweeney

Give thanks for new life and opportunities of sharing in Christ's work in unexpected places, and for the richness and diversity of life within this District.
Pray for guidance and discernment in finding effective ways of bearing witness to the gospel in the London area, with the Greater London Assembly in place;
for wisdom as we seek ways of being 'the church' where huge new developments are planned in Greenwich, Medway, North Kent Thames-side, and Ashford;
for all in the prisons and detention centres of our region;
for the continuing needs of refugees and asylum seekers who arrive in our District from many places.

London South East District

Chair:
Harvey Richardson
Secretary:
Jeremy Dare

Praying with Methodist Connexional staff

God of Wisdom, travel with us.
Open our lives, to be courageous in service;
open our eyes, to see with Christ's discernment
   that which is truly important;
open our mouths, to proclaim your Kingdom
   in our connectedness and sharing;
And may we be excited by your liberating companionship
every new day.   *Michael King, World Church Office*

Loving God,
we thank you that Christ has shown your Kingdom
to be full of possibilities;
that your love is like a rich unfolding tapestry.
Enable us to improvise so that our lives
will resonate with those possibilities too.
In the power of your Spirit
and for Christ's sake. Amen   *Harvey Richardson*

Give thanks for creative vision and inventive skill

DAY 5

Preserve us, O God, in the faith of your saints, a faith both tried and trusted. May we enjoy both now and for ever the eternal love of the Father, the abiding love of the Son and the indwelling of love of the Holy Spirit, one God in glory and majesty, world without end. Amen   *Hilary of Poitiers, 315-367*

Praying with Christians in West Africa (4)

Nigeria

Methodist Prelate:
Sunday Mbang

Mission partners:
sd Ros Colwill
ag Nigel Simpson

Give thanks for the vibrance, friendship and vitality of Nigerian Christians;
for the efforts of Wesley Guild to boost health-care facilities, including new health centres in remote areas – 'miracles in the bush'.

Pray with Nigerian people for a better understanding between the Yoruba and Hausa peoples;
for true democracy, and for the faithfulness of Christians amid increasing corruption, violence and armed robberies;
for the influence of Methodist leaders in issues of mediation with Muslims and with Shell;
for ministers who are not paid their stipends when economic problems increase;
for the caring ministry of Amaudo and Edawu where men and women with severe depression are brought from abusive situations in the streets and learn to cope with life again;
for others who are catching the vision of caring for the mentally ill and destitute.

Cameroon

Moderator of the Presbyterian Church:
Nyansako-ni-Nku

Mission partner:
th Peter Ensor°

Father, we thank you for the growth and vigour of your Church in the Cameroon. We pray that she may fulfil her calling to be 'the salt of the earth' and 'the light of the world', so that the nation as a whole may hear your voice and be transformed by the principles of your Kingdom, through Jesus Christ, your Son, our Lord.   *Peter Ensor*

Pray for the valuable work being done at the Theological College, training ministers to respond to a great hunger for the gospel.

The bread is warm and fresh,
The water cool and clear.
Lord of all life, be with us,
Lord of all life, be near.   *African grace*

Praying with Christians in Britain and Ireland

Birmingham District

Thank God for reconciliation work in Leamington Spa, combining support for the 'Bench We Share' project in Croatia and community renewal in Leamington's 'Old Town'; for District officers willingly taking extra responsibilities during the Chair's Presidential year.

Pray for ecumenical work supporting asylum-seekers, especially through 'Restore' in Birmingham and the Coventry Refugee Centre; for the District's two International Guest Houses, with their new wardens; for the Queen's Foundation and the United College of the Ascension, offering ecumenical training in ministry and mission; for all those preparing for the Connexional youth event 'Breakout', which is coming to Birmingham in July 2002.

Chair:
Christina Le Moignan
Secretary:
David Easton

Mission partners:
Florence Gundala (CSI)
Stephen and Angela Mullings, Stephanie, Angelique and Georgiane (MCCA)
th Israel* and Leelal Selvanayagam, Arul and Ani (CSI)

Creative gifts

God, Creator and Image-maker
whose Spirit is within us,
inspire us to use the gifts given by you.
Stretch our imaginations,
fire us to dream dreams
and see visions of your glory,
so that we, your church,
may spread your beauty in marvellous ways,
transforming the ordinary and everyday
into celebration and joy.
Loving God, who loves us beyond limits,
help us to spread love in your world.
Rachel Newton, Chair of the Forum for Creative Arts in Methodism

Arts in mission weekend

Gracious God,
shed your light on this day:
may the things we touch become your gifts to us,
the people we meet brothers and sisters;
may work be service
and what we suffer turn to offering;
and, dear God,
may love keep breaking through
until your Kingdom comes. Amen
Christina Le Moignan

Give thanks for God's care for people

DAY 6

To my weariness, O Lord, grant your rest; to my exhaustion, your strength and to my tired eyes, your healing light. Guide me, guard me and shelter me within the shadow of your wings and quicken me in your service with the brightness of your glory; through Jesus Christ our Lord. Amen

Lancelot Andrewes 1555-1626

Praying with Christians in Southern Africa (1)

South Africa

Presiding Bishop:
Mvume Dandala

Mission partner:
ee Rosie Venner

Botswana

Lesotho

Namibia

Swaziland

Mozambique

Bishop:
Henrique Mahlalela

Mission partners:
th/ed Peter° and
Janice Clark

Lord, Light of the world, Africa cries to you.
You are our hope for forgiveness,
healing and transformation.
Lighten our path by removing darkness from our midst.
Where there is injustice, let justice come.
Where there is war, let peace reign.
Where there is poverty, let the hungry be fed.
Where there is sickness, let disease be conquered.
May we so embrace your Holy Spirit
that we will let your Kingdom come
on earth as it is in heaven,
as we grow a society of joy, peace and righteousness.
In the name of our Lord Jesus,
Balm of Africa, Balm of the world,
we pray and dedicate ourselves,
as the Methodist people, afresh to you. Amen

Mvume Dandala

In Mozambique, we thank God,
   for the gift of reconciliation
   and pray that it may bring
   understanding between the government
   and the leader of the opposition
   in our maturing parliamentary democracy,
   and real peace for all its citizens.
We praise God,
   for mission opportunities in new regions of the country
   and give thanks for the gift of Nationals in Mission,
   and support through mission partners
   and the Methodist Relief and Development Fund.
We seek spiritual empowerment for the Church,
   as it faces the challenge of HIV/AIDS
   and absolute poverty experienced by so many
     of God's people. Amen

Henrique Mahlalela

Praying with Christians in Britain and Ireland

Give thanks for the links developing between our District and the Methodist community in King William's Town and the Phakamisa Educare Project, both in South Africa.
Pray for our new Chair and circuits planning for the future with optimism and hope.

Diversity

*I looked into the mirror to see my reflection
and saw nothing.
There, where my face should have been,
was only an empty space.
'I don't see colour,' they said.
And they didn't and I disappeared.*
O God of diversity and creative genius,
you created colour and difference so that all creation
might see your brilliance.
Help us to recognise and affirm
the uniqueness and difference that is in all humanity.

*I looked into the mirror to see my reflection
and saw pain and desolation.
There, in the mirror, was my face but it was shrouded
with contours of rejection and disappointment.
'You're not ready yet,' they said. 'Your time will come.'*
O God of love and inclusion, through the power
of your unerring eye for detail,
you see the potential
and shimmering light of greatness in all people.
May we who profess you to be Lord,
follow your example and do the same.
Give us the insight to seek out the frustrated,
the unused and those who are afraid to be used,
so that we may arm them
with your affirming and overpowering love
that is shown in Christ Jesus,
in whose name we pray. Amen
Anthony Reddie, tutor at Queen's College, Birmingham

Gracious God, in our vulnerability point us to the cross,
in our struggle for faith assure us of your presence
and in our arrogance melt our hearts by your love. Amen
Stuart J Burgess, York and Hull District

Bolton and Rochdale District

Chair:
Keith Garner
Secretary:
Paul Martin

Developing new friendships

Give thanks for God revealed in the prophets and the scriptures

DAY 7

Teach us, O Lord, to love you, to trust you and for ever to praise you. Let us exalt your name both in the day and in the night. Let us serve you both in the house of prayer and in the world about us. Let us ascribe to you with all your saints both wisdom and majesty, both honour and glory, world without end. Amen

Henry Vaughan, 1621-1695

Praying with Christians in Southern Africa (2)

Zambia

Bishop:
Patrice Siyemeto

Mission partners:
p David° and Rhoda Nixon, Samuel and Christopher
ag Jane Petty (+C of S)

Give thanks for growing congregations.
Pray for strength for the United Church to develop its vision; that its leaders and members may together explore and develop ways of becoming less dependent on external sources of support;
for the 'Life Skills' programme, training voluntary school leavers as peer educators for AIDS awareness.

God of love and power, you have promised to all who suffer
and who carry burdens that you will give us rest.
Touch and heal each of your people in our country, Zambia,
so that they may reach out in the power of the Spirit
to share your love with the peoples of the world.

Alexander Siatwinda

Zimbabwe

Bishop:
Cephas Mukandi

Mission partners:
ed Jonathan and Isobel Hill, Stephen and Susanna
p Mervyn° and Claudette Kilpatrick, Lydia, Luke, Miriam and Daniel
p Graham° and Sandie Shaw and Matthew
p Clifford° and Ruth Taylor
rt Pat Ibbotson

God of truth and love,
we praise you for this land of great beauty
  and all its sunshine peoples;
yet we grieve with you today for the tears of all who suffer
  through the mis-use of power
  and cynical manipulation of the truth.
We pray for the victims of this cruel tyranny,
and for all who are suffering in the violence
  and lawlessness that has engulfed the nation.
We give thanks for those who are working
  for peaceful change, and witnessing,
  often at great personal cost, to the power of love,
  over and against the love of power.
May your Spirit bless and guide them,
  and keep them in your truth and love,
using their service and sacrifice
  for the building of one nation which reflects your grace,
  and where all may live together in peace and harmony,
  to your praise and glory. Amen

Graham Shaw

Praying with Christians in Britain and Ireland

Enniskillen and Sligo District

Chair:
Aian Ferguson
Secretary:
Philip Agnew

Give thanks for steady work being done throughout this rural District in public worship, fellowship groups, children's and youth activities and Christian witness in the communities.
Pray that Christian people will be strengthened to witness to Jesus Christ as Saviour and Lord through word and action; that recent initiatives among children and young people will lead to many new followers of Jesus Christ; for communities suffering because of recession and difficulties in the agricultural industry.

Bristol District

Chair:
Ward Jones
Secretary:
John Carne

Rejoice in the ecumenical initiatives and outreach work being sponsored and encouraged through the Advisory Council for Social Responsibility in Gloucestershire.
Pray for the rich variety of church based work throughout the rural parts of the District;
for our newly appointed Rural Life Officer, Grace Mortimer;
for support networks serving the farming community;
for initiatives to support and enable a sense of community in village life.

Thanksgiving
Our loving Father,
we give thanks for your goodness and love;
for the joy of home and family,
and the companionship of friends and neighbours;
for the strength that supports us
and the love that surrounds us,
both when our joy is complete
and when it is touched by pain.
We give thanks for your Son Jesus Christ:
the glory of his humble birth,
the graciousness of his selfless life,
the obedience and trust that led him to the cross,
and the triumph of his resurrection and ascension.
We give thanks for your Holy Spirit
at work in your Church and in our hearts,
revealing your truth,
renewing our lives,
and bringing us to your eternal Kingdom.
Alexander Siatwinda, Zambia/Halifax

Give thanks for God's supreme revelation in Christ

DAY 8

Most holy and most loving Christ, let me behold your crown of thorns in every tear-filled eye; your bleeding and naked body in every suffering soul; your nail-pierced hands in every forgotten prisoner and your wounded feet in every lost and broken traveller; and take me to the place of my healing and theirs, even your holy cross. Amen   *Thomas Traherne, 1637-1674*

Praying with Christians in East Africa

Kenya (Tanzania and Uganda)

Presiding Bishop:
Zablon Nthamburi

Mission partners:
th/m Michael° and Heather Chester
n Barbara Dickinson
sd/d Paul and Rachel Lindoewood and Hannah
d Claire Smithson
d/n Dietmar and Birgit Ziegler, Nora, Samuel, Ronja and Jacob (+EMK)
th Caroline° and Andrew° Wickens, Matthew and Catherine (+CMS)

Loving Father, we give you **thanks and praise** for the way you have blessed the Church in Kenya, Tanzania and Uganda: for church growth, the planting of new congregations, and the building of new churches;
for ministries to alleviate poverty through rural development, primary health care and HIV/AIDS Awareness programmes;
for the ongoing work of the Methodist Hospital and the Disabled Children's Centre at Maua;
for the outstanding work among street children in Nairobi and Meru, education programmes for underprivileged children in the slums of Kibera, and the Children's Home in Kaaga.
We give thanks for the rains after the long drought and for good crops reaped in many areas: we pray for those who lost their cattle which are not so easy to replace.
We pray for the work of evangelism and outreach, in the new areas of Uganda, Tanzania and Northern Kenya, and that, as needs arise, more may hear and respond to your call to serve as doctors, nurses, social workers, agriculturists, water engineers, evangelists and ministers;
for the training of our ministers and resources to train more;
for all who serve faithfully, that they may continue with integrity and maintain the Church's witness in their communities;
for wisdom for the Church leaders as they participate in the constitutional review process in Kenya;
for a spirit of understanding and co-operation as people work together for the good of the nation, for good governance, the fight against corruption and the process towards economic recovery.   *Maureen Jones*

Praying with Christians in Wales

Give thanks for the new Community Development Trusts promoted by the Welsh Assembly in the more deprived parts of Wales, bringing together churches, police, schools, social services and other agencies to respond to local needs, particularly in relation to young people.
Pray for the farming community, the rural economy and those cruelly thrown out of work by closures in the steel industry in decaying industrial areas;
for Patrick Slattery, the new Chair of the Cymru District, and for insight and sensitivity in the future planning of Methodism in Wales;
for circuits without full-time ministers, for a real sharing of resources across Districts and with our ecumenical partners, so that the people of Wales see that the Church means something.

God of light and love, visit this land with your healing power. In your compassion restore wholeness to communities blighted by disease, destruction, and loss of hope: have mercy on your whole creation, and guide us to wise stewardship of your beautiful world, that all your creatures may live in peace and health. We ask this in the name of him in whom all things are made new, Jesus Christ our Lord. Amen
Michael Cruchley, Secretary of the Cytun Rural Network

Ysbryd byw dylifa drwom,
   Bywha dy waith a grym y groes,
Ysbryd byw, gweithia ynom,
   Cymhwysa ni i her ein hoes.
Translation of HP 777, verse 4, by E H Griffiths for the new Welsh hymn book produced by all the Free Churches and the Church in Wales – Caneuon ffydd (Gwasg Gomes, January 2001)

O Breath of life, come sweeping through us,
   Revive your church with life and power;
O Breath of life, come, cleanse, renew us,
   And fit your church to meet this hour.
Bessie Porter Head (1850-1936)

South Wales

Chair:
William Morrey
Secretary:
Jack Healey

Cymru

Chair:
Patrick Slattery
Secretary:
Dennis Griffiths

North Wales

Chair:
Barbara Bircumshaw
Secretary:
Paul Nzachahayo

Y Gymanfa

President:
Y Chwaer Eluned Williams
Secretary:
Alan Hall
Treasurer:
Anthony Gregory

Welsh banner

Give thanks for the obedience of Christ to the Father's will

Gracious God, in whom we live and move and have our being, open our eyes that we may see your fatherly presence ever about us. Teach us to be anxious for nothing and, having accomplished your holy will and purpose, to leave the outcome of all things in your most wise and loving hands; and this we ask through Jesus Christ our Lord. Amen

Richard Meux Benson, 1824-1915

Praying with Christians in South America (1)

Brazil

Bishop:
Paulo Lockmann

Give thanks for people who know the joy of celebration.
Pray with Base Christian Communities, gathering around the Bible, reflecting and praying together that they may discover how to share in the struggle for justice;
that they may continue to find mutual support and strength;
for all projects working with low-income families, reforestation, organic farming, herbal medicines, environmental education and co-operative farming;
for wisdom and strength for those who try to counteract the powerful influence of drug traffickers.

Uruguay

President:
Adolfo Tome

Give thanks for people of faith and courage.
Pray for those who are developing educational programmes for young people to increase their sense of self-worth;
for Instituto de Buena Voluntad in Montevideo, where children and young people with disabilities are cared for;
for all who minister in increasing urban slum populations and rural poverty, and among small indigenous businesses which are being replaced by multi-national companies;
for the growing relationship with the Methodist Church in Argentina.

Argentina

Bishop:
Nelly Ritchie

Mission partner:
p Sue° Jansen

Give thanks for the respect in which this Church is held, and for people who are willing to share the little they have.
Pray for church projects that are under threat because government funding is being cut;
for Solidarity Cafeteria, a Methodist project for homeless and unemployed people, where each person is known and valued and there is celebration;
for the Evangelical Centre for Social Action (now threatened by decreased funding) which offers care to single mothers, most of whom come from poor rural areas.

Praying with Christians in Britain and Ireland

Cumbria District

Chair:
David Emison
Secretary:
David Andrews

Give thanks for courage and dignity in the face of disaster;
for faith expressed in lives of integrity and goodness;
for unexpected renewal that takes us by surprise.
Pray for rural communities still recovering from the outbreak of foot-and-mouth disease;
for urban communities seeking to attract new industry and create new employment opportunities;
for church communities who are confident that life can be enriched and transformed by Jesus Christ.

Facing the future
Lord, I dared to dream,
challenges and visions of the future,
only to fall apart.
I reach rock bottom.
When I despair,
there are no easy answers,
and no clear way ahead.
Hold my hand.
Lead me beside the still waters,
restore my soul.
For you alone are the rock on which
shattered lives can be rebuilt.
I dare to dream again.
   Joy Rulton, Kirkby Stephen, Appleby and Tebay circuit

God of the morning,
as we look to the day ahead of us,
renew our trust in you.
In the daily news we hear about a world in turmoil,
and yet we know that this is your world
and that the agents of your Kingdom are at work in it.
As we look at what we plan to do today,
help us to see each task we undertake
as playing its part in fulfilling your purpose.
In every person we meet, and in every place we visit,
may we look for signs of your grace.
Help us always to respond to others
with the love that comes from you,
through Jesus Christ our Lord. Amen   *Pauline Webb*

Give thanks for the value Christ gave to human labour

DAY 10

Holy Father, we commend into your hands our family and our friends, our neighbours and our benefactors. Strengthen and confirm all faithful people and convert all sinners into your ways of goodness and love. Rouse the careless, raise the fallen, heal the sick, and grant your peace to the dying; and all for your own love's sake. Amen *Brooke Foss Westcott, 1825-1901*

Praying with Christians in South America (2)

Bolivia

Bishop:
Carlos Intipampa

Give thanks for renewed confidence;
for the bilingual text-books (supported by a Second Mile Project) now being used in primary schools.
Pray for CLEM, the women's project in Montero (supported by Network) which is planning to include a health centre;
for the women who run it – for increased confidence, mutual support and enterprise;
for the Ichatimo project helping children in a poor neighbourhood on the outskirts of Trinidad city;
that the participation of indigenous peoples will become a more integral part of the nation's life;
for viable economic alternatives to drugs (half the world's supply of cocaine is grown in Bolivia).

Peru

Bishop:
Marco A Ochoa

rt Margaret° and Aldo Valle

Give thanks for several new missions in Ica and Chincha, in spite of extensive damage caused by floods.
Pray for congregations in this area who are developing new projects including a health clinic, a youth centre, a senior citizens' centre and a new church building;
for the country as a whole at a time of political change, that military brutality and corruption may end and a more just and transparent government may emerge.

Chile

Bishop:
Neftali Aravena

Mission partners:
ed Kathryn Thomas
ee Susan Wilson and Charlotte

Give thanks that the Methodist Church is reaching at least 40,000 families.
Pray for the Church's witness through two agricultural schools and social work to encourage prisoners at Coronel to support their families;
for hope and vision in the midst of severe economic problems affecting both Church and society;
for all who continue to search for the bodies of at least 1200 people who disappeared during the dictatorship.

Praying with Christians in Britain and Ireland

Give thanks for the encouragement of fresh and continuing opportunities of witness and service through the new Clooney Hall in Londonderry and throughout the District.
Pray for those who have found a deeper faith during the year and those seeking God's will for their life in the church and in the local community.

North West District Ireland

Superintendent:
Ian Henderson
Secretary:
Harold Agnew

Give thanks for chaplaincy in the hospitals, prisons and residential homes in the islands and for links with schools and colleges.
Pray for the deacon's work among young people in St Helier and for the newly appointed workers in Alderney and Sark; for those who, by air and sea, take risks in providing the people of the islands with their daily needs.

Channel Islands District

Chair:
Ian White
Secretary:
June le Rossignol

This day's challenges
Lord, you make all things new.
Give me fresh energy to face this day's challenges
 and responsibilities.
Help me to concentrate when my mind wanders.
Prevent me from feeling guilty when I need to take time
 for myself.
Save me from pride when people praise my efforts.
Renew my desire to serve when my enthusiasm wanes.
Help me to trust you for the things I cannot change
 or understand.
Let me know your love in my life that it may touch
 others also.   *Ian Henderson*

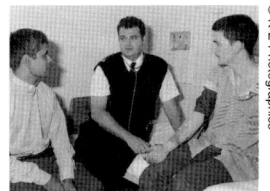

Prison chaplaincy

Lord God,
as those who are called to be your witnesses today,
we pray that we may bear witness by what we are,
by what we do and by what we say.
Give us true holiness of character,
a deeper understanding of people and their needs,
a love that is humble, outgoing and open.
So may our lives reflect something of your grace and truth
made known to us in Jesus Christ our Lord. Amen
                                              Aian Ferguson, Ireland

> **Give thanks for the strength Christ gives to his disciples**

DAY 11

Lord, you know all that lies before us, both of duty and temptation. Keep us, we pray, from all things hurtful to the body and the soul. Strengthen within us all that is praiseworthy and true, and grant that nothing may come between us and your holy presence; through Jesus Christ our Lord. Amen

John Hunter, 1849-1917

Praying with Christians in Central America

Belize and Honduras District of the MCCA

District President:
David Goff

Give thanks for the work of Wesley College which is giving many poor children a high standard of education and instilling in them Christian principles.
Pray for the work and witness of the new John and Charles Wesley Multi-purpose Centre, and for the Church's ministry in the context of child abuse, youth gangs, armed robberies, drug abuse and drug trafficking.

Panama and Costa Rica District of the MCCA

District President:
Lesley Anderson

O Lord, our God, you are the greatest, the most wonderful, truly to be appreciated and trusted in all things:
you give life to the dead,
help to the helpless, hope to the hopeless,
voice to the voiceless and strength to the weak.
We pray for Escuela Metodista de Colon,
  Escuela Metodista de Panama,
  the Valiente Indian Mission,
  the Centre for School Dropouts in Squirres, Costa Rica,
  and many other challenges facing us as a Church.
This day we give ourselves anew to you
and your service; in the name of Jesus Christ. Amen

Lesley Anderson

Guatemala

President:
Juan Pablo Ajanel

Give thanks for the Ruth and Naomi Centre, established during the time of the military conflict to generate income for widows and orphans, and for all who are encouraging women to develop new skills;
for groups who meet for biblical and theological reflection and make it a springboard for action.
Pray for all who struggle against gross inequality;
that all Christian groups may be open to change and new insights so that all may learn from one another;
for the Latin American Evangelical Centre for Pastoral Studies which works among rural communities.

Praying with Christians in Britain and Ireland

Chester and Stoke on Trent District

Give thanks for fresh initiatives in youth work in the Leek and Burslem Mission circuits.
Pray for the new Chair, John Walker, as he gets to know the District;
for the churches of the Market Drayton and Whitchurch circuits in rural Shropshire, Cheshire and Wales.

Chair:
John Walker
Secretary:
Andrew Gunstone

Service
Dear God,
remind me that every moment of my life is precious,
so that I may use my time doing those things
which bring me closer to you.
Teach me how to serve you,
to give joyously, to share willingly and to love totally.
Remind me that I cannot serve
when greed, doubt, fear or anger fill my mind.
Fill me with your light
so that your blessings will shine through me into the world.
Each day, as I awake, be present in my thoughts
and may every moment of my life be a channel
through which some measure of your love and light
may reach others.
A young person, Bethel circuit, Barbados

Living Lord,
humanity and creation, when touched by you,
come alive in exciting and often unexpected ways.
In those moments when we are conscious of
human frailty or limitation,
the struggle to make sense of life,
being uncertain where next to turn,
may we be alert to you and allow
your thoughts to stir our spirit,
your mind to encompass our thinking,
and your will to engage our will.
Ward Jones, Bristol

Give thanks for the call to follow Christ

DAY 12

Holy Spirit of God, let us not seek you in the distant land, for you are here among us. Let us welcome you in the heart which is your dwelling place and let us rejoice in the glory of your presence, the only fountain of goodness and love. Amen
Amy Carmichael, 1868-1951

Praying with Christians in the Caribbean (1)

Methodist Church in the Caribbean and the Americas (MCCA)

Connexional President: Bruce Swapp

We thank God for relationships with others, reminding us of the universal nature of God's mission and work; for the dedication and courage of so many in seeking the lost, reclaiming the lapsed, supporting the weak and strengthening one another in the faith.
Bruce Swapp

Guyana District

District President: Barrington Litchmore

Creator God, our District theme, 'Calling God's People to Reconciliation and Celebration', challenges us to the realities of brokenness within ourselves, our families and our nation. As you were in Christ reconciling the world to yourself, so you call us to this work of healing. With thanksgiving, we joyously anticipate the Bicentenary of Methodist witness in Guyana in 2002, with thanks for the increasing commitment of young people and the gifts and abilities of all who lead us in mission.
Barrington Litchmore

Leeward Islands District

District President: Selwyn Vanterpool

God our Father, we praise you that we can station a presbyter in the Guadeloupe and Martinique Mission and are opening the much-needed Resource Centre; and for progress made with Holland Mission. Bless these and other outreach initiatives being launched in 2001/2002. Protect our region and be with us as we minister amid the HIV/AIDS epidemic, escalating crime and moral decline; through Jesus Christ our Lord. Amen
Selwyn Vanterpool

South Caribbean District

District President: Anne Daniel

Mission partner:
p Elaine Thomas°

Raise us up, O Lord, to meet the challenges of the present age. We feel ill-equipped. Show us how to minister to vagrants without being patronising. They are broken, Lord, they have lost connectedness with you and their fellow human beings. They need a sense of belonging. Guide us to know when to touch them spiritually and emotionally. Enable us to respond, no matter how painful may be the experience, in Jesus' name. Amen
Anne Daniel

Praying with Christians in Britain and Ireland

Give thanks for change but not decay: change in many buildings renewed for mission, the local ecumenical partnership finally building at Tregadillett, the new church built at Tamar Valley, and change in so many flexible forms of ministry developing among us.

Pray for Chris Blake, Joy, Anna and Stephen, our new District Chair and his family;
for Roger Greene and his new work as County Chaplain to Agriculture, our District Evangelism Enabler, Steve Wild, and our Training and Development Officer, David Rhymer, as they continue their excellent work. May they grow and work together as a team.

For local preachers

Jesus the carpenter, we pray for those you have called
from different backgrounds of work and leisure
to preach your Word.
May their message, given by your Spirit
and forged in daily experience,
be relevant, vital and inspiring
to all who hear, see and know them.
Encouraging Lord,
we pray for all who are testing their call to preach
and for those with years of experience and service,
that together they may find inspiration,
fellowship, mutual support and grow in faith
as they proclaim the good news of Jesus Christ.
Risen Lord, when commitment and inspiration burn low,
deepen their awareness of your living presence
that brings the life, newness and joy
to be proclaimed in your name
and through the power of the Holy Spirit. Amen
Edward Pender, local preacher, Redhill

Lord of love and greatest might,
Lord of all – in holiest height,
Lord in whom is all delight;
    Keep us ever in your sight,
    Set our stubborn hearts alight,
    Help us to reflect your light,
Lord of everlasting light. Amen
Garth Waite, Falmouth

Cornwall District

Chair:
Chris Blake
Secretary:
Howard Curnow

Buildings renewed for mission

Give thanks for opportunities of work and leisure

DAY 13

Be light to my eyes, O Lord, and music to my ears. Be to me sweetness of taste and contentment of heart. Be sunshine to me in the day, food at my table and repose in the night. I give to you, O Lord, my body and my soul, all that I have and all that I am; my fame, my friends, my liberty and my life. Dispose of me according to your gracious will and the glory of your holy name; through Christ our Lord. Amen

John Cosin, 1594-1672

Praying with Christians in the Caribbean (2)

Jamaica District

District President:
Philip Robinson

Mission partners:
p/p Conrad° and Sonia° Hicks, Nathan, Olivia and Nyasha

Give thanks for scenes of natural beauty – mountains, hills, plains, valleys, streams, forests, fruit trees, flowers – reminders of how God has richly blessed the land.
Pray that more young men and women might respond to the call of God to full-time service;
that those in local leadership may find more creative ways to address the problems – unemployment, crime, violence, drug-trafficking and substance abuse.
May all work towards achieving the goal of our nation's motto: 'Out of many, one people'.

George Mulrain

Bahamas and Turks and Caicos Islands District

District President:
Raymond R Neilly

Give thanks for political stability and economic prosperity.
Pray that the continuing rift in the District may be overcome in a spirit of openness and desire for reconciliation;
for Derek Browne, a National in Mission in Andros, who is developing a co-operative, family life programmes and a multi-purpose resource centre to offer courses in leadership, vocational training and child-care.

Haiti District

District President:
Raphael Dessieu

Give thanks for people of hope and growing churches;
for the Methodist Church's rural development programme, benefiting 200,000 people, through environmentally sound techniques, literacy, animal husbandry... overcoming poverty, helping people to help themselves.
Pray for candidates offering for the ministry;
for the Church's mission in the context of economic difficulties;
for Haitians now living in poverty in the Dominican Republic where they are denied basic human rights;
for a closer relationship between the Methodist Church in Haiti and the Dominican Evangelical Church.

Praying with Christians in Britain and Ireland

North East District Ireland

Superintendent:
Paul Kingston
Secretary:
Roy Cooper

Give thanks for the encouragement received through the Alpha course in many circuits, and for those who have come to faith. May they continue in a life of discipleship.
Pray for an end to all sectarian violence in the District; for everyone who is seeking to share God's love and break down the barriers of hate and suspicion; for David Rock in his new appointment as Connexional Youth Secretary; for those working with young people that they may know an abundance of God's grace each new morning.

Darlington District

Chair:
Graham Carter
Secretary:
Ian Scott

Give thanks for new ecumenical opportunities arising throughout the District where people are taking the life and mission of the Church seriously; for the development of Tees Valley Ministries, as they take on the role of industrial mission and working with communities affected by changes in working life.
Pray for our rural communities as they reassess their life in the aftermath of foot-and-mouth disease; for the new work in Ingleby Barwick, the largest housing estate in Europe, and the developing work in Middlesbrough town centre.

God of yesterday,
we thank you, for you have been with us
through the good and bad,
even when we have not recognised you.
God of today,
we seek your presence now;
help us to open our eyes and look in the right places.
God of tomorrow,
we trust you for what is to come;
give us the confidence to follow in your way.
God of all times and all places,
each new day is yours;
renew our lives day by day in your service,
for Christ's sake. Amen

Graham Carter

Mural for ex-mining community, Darlington

Give thanks for the truths God has enabled humanity to discover

DAY 14

Make us worthy, O Lord, to serve our sisters and brothers throughout the world. Through us draw near to all who live and die in poverty and hunger. Give to them through our hands the bread they need for today and the love and joy and peace which is life in you, now and always. Amen

Mother Teresa of Calcutta, 1910-1996

Praying with Christians in North America

United Methodist Church (USA)

Ecumenical Officer to the Council of Bishops: Sharon Zimmerman Rader

Give thanks for openness to people of different opinions, cultural traditions and ethnic backgrounds.
Pray with the United Methodist Church as it helps people who are experiencing emotional stress and searching for meaning. May the current theme, 'Our hearts, our minds and our doors are always open' inspire a greater sense of belonging and support to all in need.
Pray for the Government;
for President Bush – that he will allow his Christian faith to speak to the daily job of being President and America's leadership in global issues.

The United Church of Canada

General Secretary: Virginia Coleman

O God, you have spoken to us through the story of Ruth, sojourner in a foreign land, and were yourself present among us in Jesus to gather and welcome all those who were cast out and adrift from their societies; stir us and speak to us afresh through the migrant people of our time.

Adapted from 'Gathering' (United Church of Canada)

Awaken in us with each day,
new hopes, new dreams of colours,
loves and joys never before imagined.

Fill our bodies with your breath; invigorate us.
Carry us to the farthest mountains and beyond.

In-spirit us that we might reach out to you boldly
to grasp the miracles that are given with each new dawn.

'Prayer to the Four Winds'
From 'Native American Leaders Make a Difference'
(General Board of Discipleship)

Praying with Christians in Britain and Ireland

Give thanks for refurbished churches as signs of the Kingdom of God in cities, towns and villages.
Pray for commitment to sustaining the life of rural communities; for farmers, growers and consumers, that they may play their part effectively in the local food economy;
for people working in chaplaincies as they support the ministry of the whole people of God in the world.

East Anglia District

Chair:
Malcolm Braddy
Secretary:
Diana Sawyer

Praying with children
Dear God, you give us children
for fun, for hope, for challenge,
as patterns of discipleship.
But often we fail our children and lose our dream.

You give us children, who have the right to a name,
who need to feel they are wanted.
But many never belong to anyone.

You give us children,
who need adequate nutrition and medical care.
But some get a great deal,
while others suffer from malnutrition and disease.

You give us children, who sometimes have disabilities,
who need special care.
But we keep them dependent
  and their gifts go unrecognised.

You give us children who need nurture and love,
who need protection from harm.
But some are neglected and others are abused.

Dear God, you give us children.
Let us value our children and find our dream.
Judy Jarvis, Child Protection Office

Lord, grant us space today,
To pause,
To pray,
To act in harmony with you. Amen   *Malcolm Braddy*

Give thanks for the intercession of Christ in heaven

Asia

May we rid our minds
of greed, anger,
and delusion,
so that we become
centres of
peacefulness,
reaching out to others.
May those we meet
feel the sincerity
of our intentions,
so that they may also
radiate the love
which alone
destroys hatred.

Buddhist prayer

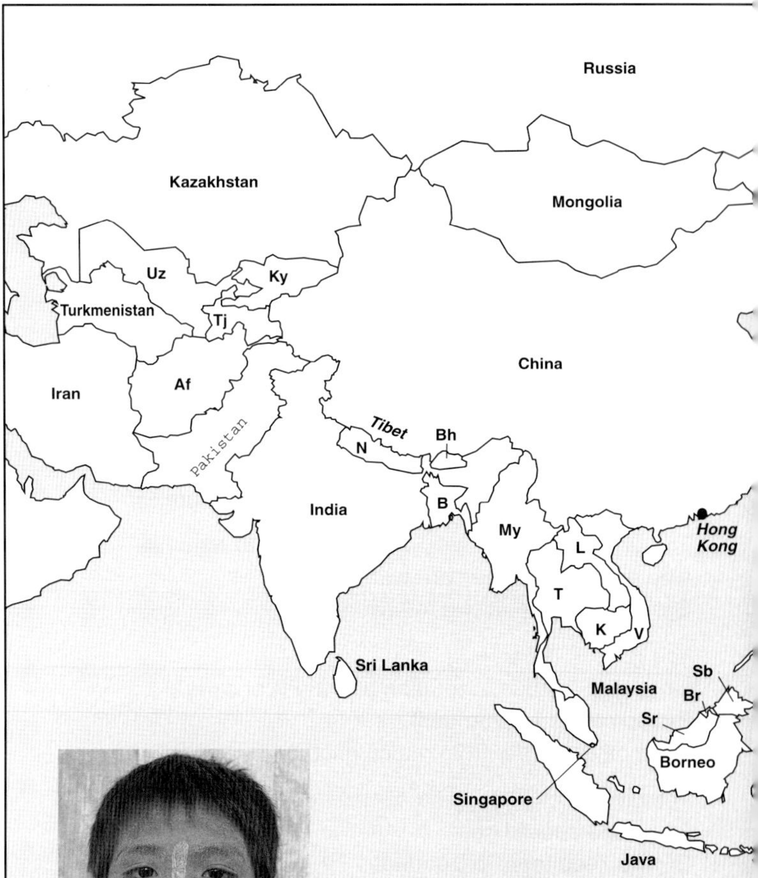

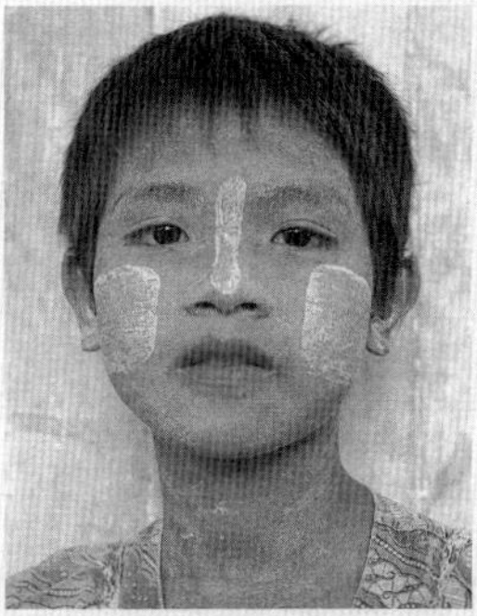
Burma

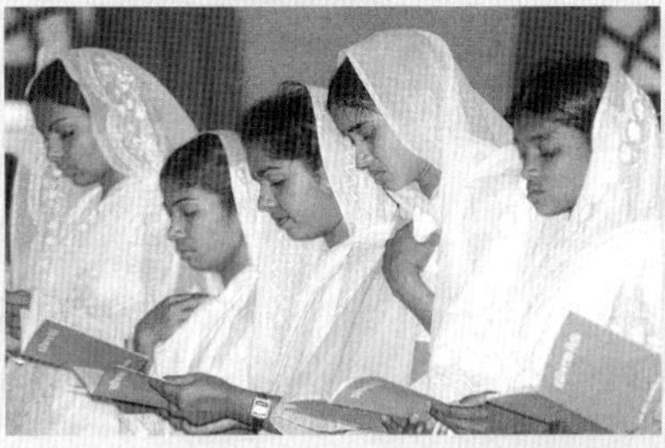
North India

India

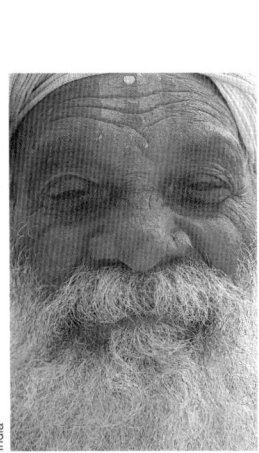

The Pacific

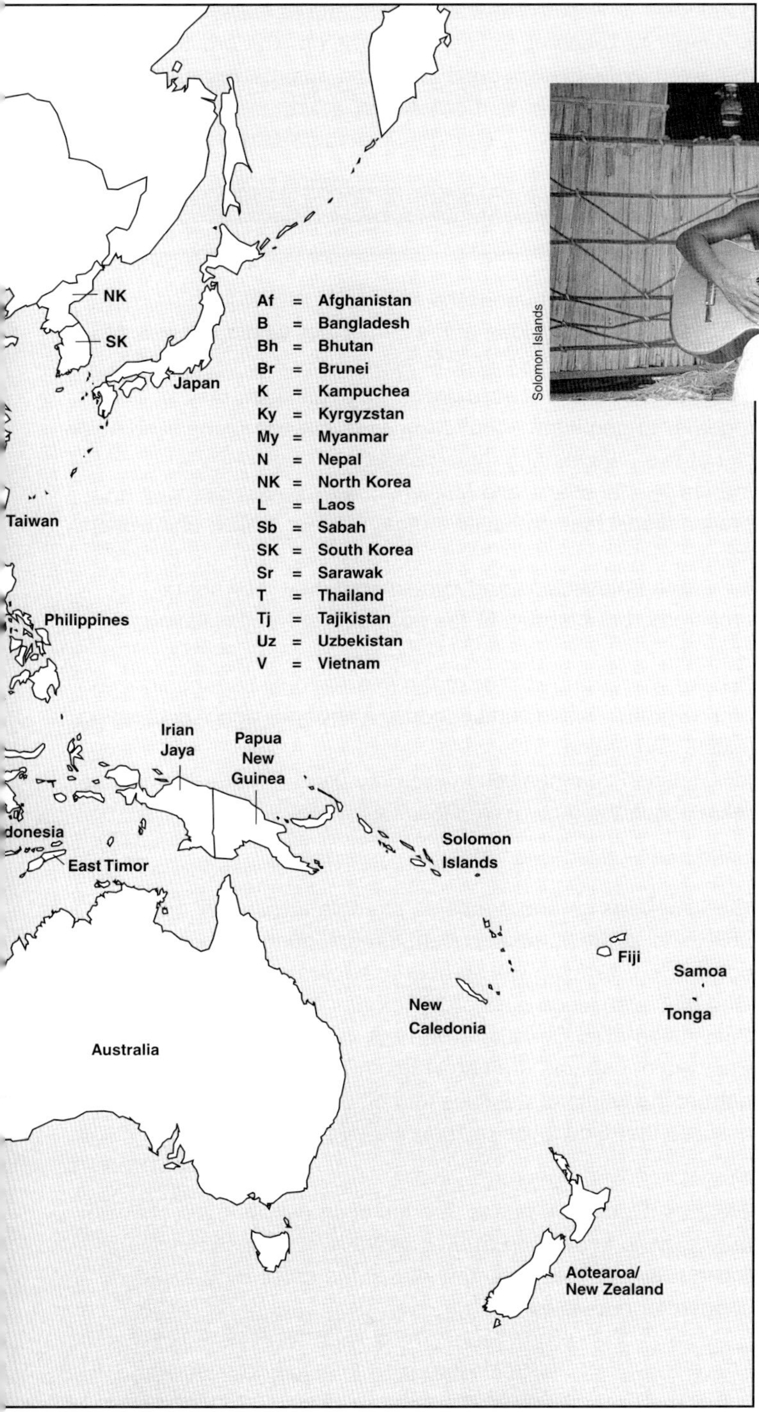

NK
SK
Japan
Taiwan
Philippines
Irian Jaya
Papua New Guinea
donesia
East Timor
Solomon Islands
Fiji
Samoa
Tonga
New Caledonia
Australia
Aotearoa/ New Zealand
Af = Afghanistan
B = Bangladesh
Bh = Bhutan
Br = Brunei
K = Kampuchea
Ky = Kyrgyzstan
My = Myanmar
N = Nepal
NK = North Korea
L = Laos
Sb = Sabah
SK = South Korea
Sr = Sarawak
T = Thailand
Tj = Tajikistan
Uz = Uzbekistan
V = Vietnam

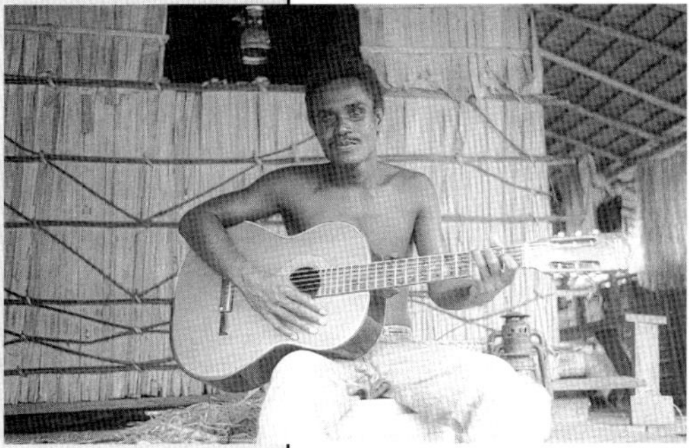

Solomon Islands

Lord,
oil the hinges
of our heart's doors
that they may swing
gently and easily
to welcome you.

Papua New Guinea

China

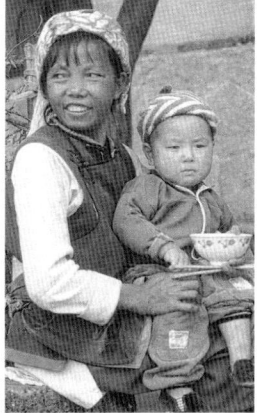

DAY 15

O Lord, whose way is perfect, help us always to trust in your goodness, to walk in the way of faith, and to follow in the path of simplicity. Teach us to cast our cares on your providence, that we may possess a quiet mind and a contented spirit; through Jesus Christ our Lord. Amen

Christina Georgina Rossetti, 1830-1894

Praying with Christians in the Middle East

The Holy Land

Pray for all who live under the sounds of rocket-fire;
for families on both sides of the conflict for whom this is a time of mourning;
'Pray for the peace of Jerusalem...' that all sides may sit down together to negotiate – that Jerusalem may be recognised as a city of two peoples and three faiths;
that Jews, Christians and Muslims may, through dialogue and prayer, dispel fear and build mutual respect, peace and welfare for all;
for young Palestinians and Israelis that they may not be embittered but be open to the possibility of reconciliation and change;
that we who are members of the international community may empower the United Nations to be a stronger agent in bringing justice and peace;
for Christian communities in the Holy Land – that hope may be rekindled in the face of all difficulties...

'God supports us and grants us strength through all our afflictions, distress, persecution, famine, hunger, and oppression. 'Nothing will be able to separate us from the love of God in Christ Jesus our Lord' (Romans 8.35). And thus we Palestinian Arab Christians who live in Palestine and the Middle East are not spared the hardships of humankind. Yet, if we entrust the whole of our lives into God's hands then we will be assured that God loves us, and the sun will shine on us.'

Aida Haddad

'Help us, God, as we pass through such difficult trials, that we may grow to know your truth, that we may witness to you our Saviour by our lives. May the way of the cross be the one we choose for ourselves...'

Najwa Farah
From 'The Things That Make For Peace',
Sabeel Liberation Theology Group, Jerusalem

Praying with Christians in Britain and Ireland

Give thanks for new people coming into the life of the Church through initiatives like 'Walk Isle of Man', 'Alpha' and the 'Millennium Candle Project' during the Millennium Year.
Pray for Malcolm Peacock, the new Superintendent in the Ramsey circuit, for Stewardship programmes in the Douglas and Peel circuit, and for the Creative Arts Project in the Castletown circuit.

Isle of Man District
Rheynn Ellan Vannin Yn Agglish Haasilagh

Chair:
Stephen Caddy
Secretary:
Irene Robinson

We bow our heads in worship of the Father
We bow our heads in worship of the Son
We bow our heads in worship of the Spirit
We worship you, O God, the Three in One.

We bow our heads in shame for careless speaking
We bow our heads in shame for selfish thought
We bow our heads in shame for foolish actions
And for those times your Kingdom passed unsought.

We bow our heads receiving your forgiveness
We close our eyes to feel your healing touch
We still our hands within this sacred moment
We wait for grace that gives to us so much.

We say Amen. Amen to God the Father
We say Amen. Amen to God the Son
We say Amen. Amen now Holy Spirit
Amen. Amen. Amen. Your will be done.
Stephen Caddy

O God, who holds the whole world in your hands, help me – in my prayers, in my work and through such help as I can offer – to embrace the whole world with you, knowing that no place is too small for your concern, and no map too large for me to live on, for Jesus Christ's sake. Amen
Pauline Webb

> **Give thanks for the joy of human love and friendship**

DAY 16

Set our hearts on fire with love for you, O Christ, that in its flame we may love the Lord our God with all our heart, mind, soul and strength and in this holy fire we may love our neighbours as ourselves; that in the keeping of these holy commandments we may glorify your name, now and for ever. Amen

Orthodox prayer

Praying with Christians in the Indian Subcontinent

Church of Bangladesh

Bishop of Dhaka:
Dwijen Mondal

Mission partners:
n Gillian Rose
th/ad+ Andrew° and Rosemary Symonds
th/ed+ John° and Rita Bennett
p+ Anne Tuesley
(all joint appointments with CofS, CMS, USPG, MCB)

Thank you, Lord, for this beautiful country,
Sonar Bangla (golden Bengal),
this ever-green delta country with many wide rivers,
hot summers, heavy monsoon rains, pleasant winters,
fertile fields with golden paddies, lush vegetation.
Thank you for the gifts
of many of your great sons and daughters,
spiritual leaders, saints, intellectual giants,
poets and writers;
and for many simple folk –
for their songs and dance and a rich culture.
Ours is a friendly and hospitable people,
living in closely-knit families.
You know, Lord, we also suffer a lot,
our small sorrows and big problems
that arise from overpopulation, wars, floods,
cyclones, land erosion and joblessness.
Many go hungry: children and older people;
mothers die in child-birth
in a world where this need not be.
Our young people write their dreams on the walls:
'a world without any visas',' a world belonging to all'.
Let this new Millennium bring fulfilment
and salvation from every bondage, your salvation, Lord.

Dwijen Mondal

Church of Pakistan

Moderator:

Almighty God,
whose Son came to earth
to dwell with the lowly and simple,
with the victims of violence and crisis,
and with the outcasts and rejected of society;
may we keep the same company.

*From 'Procession of Prayers',
ed. John Carden (Cassell)*

Praying with Christians in Britain and Ireland

Leeds District

Give thanks for the new youth drop-in centre and study support project in the rural Pateley Bridge circuit and for the Rank Trust funding which has made it possible.
Pray that the Church Life Audit undertaken by the Training and Development Officers for the whole District may prove useful in determining how to move forward in mission and ministry; for lay worker Rosemary Nicholls in the Castleford circuit as she exercises a ministry alongside bereaved people.

Chair:
Michael Townsend
Secretary:
John Santry

Belfast District

Give thanks for growth and development in teaching and in youth and children's work;
for the vision and sacrifice of congregations who have appointed lay people to work with ministers to respond to new opportunities for the Kingdom.
Pray for circuits suffering the effects of urban change;
for David Neilands as he takes up his new appointment as chaplain of Methodist College;
for Dennis Cooke, Principal of Edgehill College in this important year of building and refurbishment, and for all who work with him in preparing people for ministry;
for men and women who want to serve God, that they may see opportunities for faith sharing and faith building within the ordained ministry and be open to hear God's call.

Superintendent:
Brian Fletcher
Secretary:
David Mullan

God of new beginnings,
your love to us knows neither measure nor end.
Reveal yourself to us in the ordinary things of life,
so that each day's tasks may be done for love of you
and each day's living may bring us nearer you;
through Jesus Christ, your Son, our Saviour.
Michael Townsend

As our tropical sun gives forth its light,
so let the rays from your face enter
every nook of my being
and drive away all darkness within.
The Philippines

Give thanks for our families and friends

DAY 17

Grant us grace, O God, lightly to bear our joys and sorrows; love that we may be fruitful in your service; compassion never to disown the poor and courage never to yield to insolent might. Raise our minds above earthly trifles and our spirits to the place where you live and reign in glory, now and for ever. Amen

Rabindranath Tagore, 1861-1941

Praying with Christians in India

Church of North India (CNI)

Moderator:
James Terom

Give thanks for the sustained unity of the Church of North India, in spite of internal and external threats.
Pray for the victims of the devastating earthquake in Gujarat State, and for the Church which, along with many others, has been deeply involved in relief and rehabilitation work;
for the comforting of victims themselves who will have to find new meaning for their lives;
for the political stability of our country and region;
for God's grace for those who divide people on the basis of caste, creed or religion;
for *Dalits* who struggle against discrimination – may God guide those in power to bring justice to them so that they also may taste life in its fullness;
for world peace – may the Prince of Peace establish his Kingdom where peace, justice and the integrity of creation flow like the water of life.

V/S Lall, General Secretary of the CNI Synod

Church of South India (CSI)

Moderator:
K J Samuel

Mission partners:
sd Margaret Addicott
p+ Eileen Thompson°
(+CofS, USPG, Oxford Mission)
ee Janet Hastings

Loving Father, thank you for the Church of South India.
For its witness as a United and a Uniting Church,
we lift up our hearts to you.
We pray for its commitment to take up the cause
of girl children who are often deprived
of basic comforts just because they are female.
May we be a channel of your grace.
We also remember the CSI's commitment to the *dalits*
(those who belong to the lowest strata of society)
and the *adivasis* (tribals).
May this mission, to lift up under-privileged people,
pave the way for a more humane world.
Bless this ministry for the sake of your Kingdom.
In Jesus' name, we pray. Amen.

Office of the CSI

Praying with Christians in Britain and Ireland

Give thanks for courage, creativity and vision welling up within the life of the District, ground-breaking ecumenical initiatives at all levels, especially the mission partnership between the Brigg and Barton circuits and the Yarborough Deanery.
Pray for our circuit leadership teams initiating and managing change;
for the Growing in Ministry (GIM) group for those in their first five years of ministry;
for our rural communities struggling with crisis, our agricultural chaplain – Alan Robson – and the Lincolnshire Rural Stress Network;
for the Forge drop-in project in the Scunthorpe circuit;
for the work of the District through the newly established unit structure;
and for the new Bishop of Lincoln.

Lincoln and Grimsby District

Chair:
David Perry
Secretary:
Christopher Humble

Praying with women
We pray for women who are victims of cruelty,
injustice and neglect;
for women in conflict situations and war zones;
for those under the constant threat of abuse and rape,
and for those in unlawful detention.
Give them courage and strength to endure,
and peace and love to forgive their enemies.
Bind us together with your thread of hope and mercy.
Bring the world, O God, to look into your face of love
and grant us the help of your Spirit
in our prayers for the salvation of all people.
In Jesus' name we pray.
Amen   *Kathleen Fowlis and Matilda Johnson,*
    Women's Committee of the South Caribbean District

Through the cracks in hard-baked earth,
between fault lines of failure and neglect,
into the place of our longing and searching:
Let your wellsprings rise and burst forth
transfiguring the landscape;
refreshing souls; renewing hope;
nourishing tender shoots of new ways of being,
O fierce and gentle source of living water.
            Liz Smith, Market Rasen and Caistor circuit

Give thanks for the peace of God which passes all understanding

DAY 18

Here, O Lord, is my poor heart, an empty vessel ready to be filled with your grace. Here, O Lord, is my sinful soul, waiting to be refreshed by your love. Here, O Lord, is my mouth created for your praise and ready to proclaim the glory of your name, now and for ever. Amen   *Dwight Lyman Moody, 1837-1899*

Praying with Christians in Asia

Myanmar/Burma
The Methodist Church of Upper Myanmar

Methodist President: Haokhojam

Pray that we may not forget the suffering people of Burma;
for the many prisoners of conscience and political prisoners, that they may hold on to hope and their vision of freedom;
for the growing number of refugees into Northern Thailand;
for political change without violence and for Aung San Suu Kyi;
for greater international pressure to effect change and democracy;
for health workers in remote rural areas;
that the lonely and isolated may know that they are upheld by prayer.

Nepal: The United Mission to Nepal (UMN)

Director of the UMN: Jennie Collins

Mission partners:
ag Finlay and Rachel Hodge, Elizabeth and Peter
ed+ Paul and Sarah Wright and Jack

INF Mission partners: Peter and Lynda Jaques (International Nepal Fellowship)

Give thanks for progress and development in Church and society in Nepal in the past.
Pray for reconciliation and harmony in politics and among church groups so that progress and development may continue.   *Ruth Angove*

Father God, we pray for Nepal and its Hindu and Buddhist population, that they will experience your love. Strengthen the growing Nepali Church in its fellowship and ministry. We pray for the work of the United Mission to Nepal and its staff, expatriates and Nepalis, who seek to minister to the people's needs in your name. Encourage more doctors, teachers and other professionals to respond to your call to fill the urgent vacancies in UMN programmes. Bless the many programmes carried out in rural development, education, health, engineering and industrial development. Bless our new Director, Jennie Collins, in the process of redefining the UMN's mission and leading it into the future.   *Stefan Ostman*

Praying with Christians in Britain and Ireland

Give thanks for creative and imaginative work being done by the NCH in Warrington in the Butterfly Project;
for the challenge to work with young people represented by the Kidz Club in Huyton.
Pray for Merseyside's ecumenical 'Mission in the Economy' as it seeks new ways of working;
for those ministers on sabbatical leave, that they may be renewed in vision;
for those who have no work and who struggle to find direction in life;
for those made redundant and whose world has collapsed around them;
for those who suffer from status loss because they no longer have any paid employment;
for those who continue to be bereaved, who may not have a body to bury, whose grief remains an open sore because they fail to find proper 'closure'.

Liverpool District

Chair:
John Taylor
Secretary:
Neil Stubbens

The Word
Thank you, God,
For shared words:
Words that make us think,
Words that leave us wondering,
Words that put us right,
Words that inspire.

The greeting of strangers,
The conversation of friends,
Our mother tongue,
Your gospel Word.

Words that make us laugh,
Words that move us to tears,
Words that encourage,
Words that heal,
Words that speak the truth in love.

Thank you, God,
For shared words –
And shared silences.
   Jan S Pickard, Warden of the Iona Community

Give thanks for our share in Christ's ministry of reconciliation

DAY 19

Lord Jesus Christ, whose arms of love were stretched wide upon the cross so that all may come within your saving embrace; stretch forth in mercy the hands of your Church today that in its ministry of compassion we may enter again into the Kingdom of your justice and grace. Amen

Charles Henry Brent, 1862-1929

Praying with Christians in Asia

Sri Lanka

Methodist President:
Noel Fernando

Mission partners:
lib Margaret Julian (+USPG)
p/m David° and Sue Palmer

Father, Creator, Judge of all humankind,
thank you for the love, care and spiritual guidance
we receive through the fellowship of the Church;
for the sharing of joys, and for opportunities
to share the sorrows of all who are affected by war,
natural disasters, disease and hunger.

We praise you for the courage of our brothers and sisters
who hold to your love and grace
as they suffer in war-torn areas.

Lord, make the Church a powerful influence for good
before the rulers and the rebellious of our land,
that together we may pray and seek your face
so that our country is healed.

Lord, help us to be conscious of deliberate acts
of persecution in this part of the world.
Lift up those who are afflicted
and make them strong and unwavering in faith.

Give us wisdom to preserve your beautiful creation
for the benefit of future generations.

In the name of Jesus Christ, our living Saviour.
Amen
Sunil Warnakulasuriya

Indonesia and East Timor

Gereja Methodista
Bishop:
H H Doloksaribu

Pray for the fragile Indonesian democracy;
for the Maluku islands that they may regain the harmony for which they were once known;
for an end to repression and the violation of human rights;
for justice and integrity in business dealings;
for the people of East Timor still suffering abuse and arbitrary death, and for churches who serve them.
Where violence and the suffering of the innocent seem endless, we pray that hopefulness, acts of love and sharing may finally overcome the powers that bring death.

Praying with Christians in Britain and Ireland

Manchester and Stockport District

Chair:
David Willie
Secretary:
Fred Bell

Give thanks for the varied forms of ministry offered by presbyters, deacons, lay workers, circuit and local church officers as they respond to the challenge of serving Christ in their communities.

Pray for the new Manchester circuit and the new Salford circuit as they explore different opportunities for mission in the city centre and in urban areas;

for representatives from the District and the Manchester Diocese as they plan a Joint Synod to receive the final report of the Formal Conversations between the Church of England and the Methodist Church;

for the 'More than Gold' initiative in preparation for the Commonwealth Games and for the Churches' role in the regeneration of East Manchester.

The city

Give thanks to God for the life of the city:
>for the wealth of the city,
>its busy work life,
>its opportunities for leisure,
>the rich variety of peoples and cultures,
>and for new homes in the city.

Pray to God for the life of the city:
>for the great gap between the rich and the poor;
>for those made redundant
>>and those who have never known work;
>
>for those whose lives are dominated by drink
>>and drugs;
>
>for the tensions between those of different cultures;
>for those without a place to live.

Loving God,
enable us to redeem the life of the city,
that all shall be able to share the richness of its life.
David Weeks, Bristol

> **Give thanks for all who are agents of Christ's compassion**

DAY 20

Teach us, O Lord, to serve you with patience, to follow you with simplicity, to reverence you with fear and to love you with our whole heart; that serving, following, reverencing and loving we may behold you in the beauty of holiness and rest in the presence of your glory, now and for ever. Amen

Evelyn Underhill, 1875-1941

Praying with Christians in Asia

Singapore

Bishop:
Robert Solomon

Give thanks for the challenges of a cosmopolitan, multi-faith population.
Pray for mutual respect and social harmony;
for those who are left behind and forgotten in this flourishing, commercial centre;
for self-help groups offering hope and new beginnings;
for those who are censured by the Government if they challenge the status quo;
for all who are oppressed by pressure to succeed;
for free speech and open debate about the issues that affect society;
for mission across cultures.

Malaysia

Resident Bishop:
Peter Chio Sing Ching

Special assignment:
th David and Rhona Burfield

Give thanks for political stability and harmony in this multi-cultural and multi-religious nation;
for freedom of belief in this country where Islam is the official religion;
for the rapid growth of the Church – the result of local Christians sharing the good news.
Pray for wisdom and sensitivity as Christians seek to proclaim the gospel to all peoples;
for the reprinting and distribution of the Bible in Malay;
for the calling and training of pastors and church workers who will become the future leadership;

Cambodia

OMF Mission partner:
Naomi Sharp

for a balanced proclamation of the gospel which brings wholeness – spiritually, physically, emotionally, mentally and socially;
for growth of mission concern to plant God's Kingdom beyond the borders of Malaysia;
for clear and attractive biblical teaching in the churches to complement the Charismatic renewal.

David Burfield

Praying with Christians in Britain and Ireland

Newcastle Upon Tyne District

Chair:
Leo Osborn
Secretary:
John Williams

Mission partners:
Sipho° and Zime Nyembezi, Nkululeko, Nondumiso, Nosipho and Nokwazi

Give thanks and **pray** for the Tynedale circuit, bringing together Allendale, Haltwhistle and Hexham, for the new superintendent and all who work with him in that widespread circuit of rural Northumberland;
for the newly formed North East Churches Together, that it may support and encourage deepening ecumenical relationships;
for churches and individuals involved in the care of refugees and asylum seekers, that strangers in our midst may feel welcomed and understood.
Pray for our new District Chair, Leo Osborn, as he takes on the tasks of leadership and care.

Praying with young people

Loving God, thank you for youth groups and their leaders.
Refresh, renew and encourage
all who work with the Church to empower the young.
Thank you for churches where young people have a role,
and that you bless them as they carry out your mission.
We pray for young people who feel alone
and alienated by the Church,
especially those in the 18-30 age group.
May the Church become more approachable
so that they feel they belong,
that they are valued for their faith and for themselves.
We ask that, through our experience of your love
and our work with young people,
we may learn to accept and to learn from one another
that we may begin to change the Church and the world.
Through Jesus Christ. Amen
The Methodist Youth Executive

Almighty and ever-loving God,
we offer ourselves again to you.
Help us and guide us in today's times of busyness
and times of quiet.
Help us to be thoroughly yours in all things.
Help us to be humble yet wise,
to be able to pursue the truth with kindness
and to listen and learn from those around us.
Guide and direct us in all this we pray. Amen *Wesley Blakey*

Give thanks for all opportunities to proclaim the gospel

DAY 21

Grant to me, O Lord, a humble, lowly and quiet heart. Give to my waking hours patience, kindness and tenderness of soul. Let all my words, my works and my thoughts be overshadowed by the gift of your most Holy Spirit, now and for ever. Amen
Thomas More, 1478-1535

Praying with Christians in the Far East

China

President of China Christian Council:
Han Wenzao

Amity staff:
Ian Groves
Amity teachers:
Eileen Brodie
Richard Brunt
Stuart Craig
Mick and Anne
  Kavanagh
Sarah Ker
Richard Lester
Mark McLeister
Vera Vicente

Hong Kong (Special Administrative Region of China)

Methodist President:
Li Ping-Kwong

Crowded on subways,
  labouring on building sites,
    toiling in rice-fields,
serving in shops,
  working in factories,
    teaching in schools,
relaxing in pool halls,
  lounging on streets,
    training for Olympics,
computing in offices,
  governing in ministries,
    trading in markets,
performing in theatres,
  strolling in parks,
    praying in temples,
exercising, chatting, cycling, cooking,
  eating, learning, loving, burying...
Behold the people of China – your people.

We pray for their health and safety,
  for the conscientious management of all workplaces.
We pray for economic and judicial systems
  where neither rewards nor punishments are excessive.
We pray that rulers and people alike may be free
  of both fear and greed
and for peaceful international partnership with China
  in all walks of life.

We ask God's blessing
on the churches throughout China, including Hong Kong;
on over-stretched and under-resourced pastors;
on those who define and refine,
test and contest the relations between Church and State.
John Pritchard, Chair of Friends of the Church in China

Praying with Christians in Britain and Ireland

Down District

Chair:
Robin Roddie
Secretary:
Thomas Deacon

Give thanks for co-operation among churches in mission through imaginative initiatives to the whole community in Lisburn and the joint Church of Ireland/Methodist Movilla Abbey church in Newtownards;
for new adventures in Christian service through youth teams and pastors in Holywood, Bangor, and Lisburn.
Pray for the Link project in Newtownards, combating youth delinquency and drug addiction;
for the work of Methodism in the Bangor area as discussions take place to look at the future of three separate circuits working more closely together.

North Lancashire District

Chair:
Stephen Poxon
Secretary:
Andrew Horsfall

Give thanks for circuits responding to the challenges of being the Church in new ways;
for congregations who are willing to come together to strengthen their witness to God's love, especially in Lancaster, Clayton le Moors and the new ecumenical circuit in Darwen.
Pray for those churches that are working within their communities as an outworking of the gospel of Christ;
for the newly opened First Steps Community Centre at North Shore, Blackpool, the new Building Bridges inter-faith project centre in Nelson, and growing work in the villages of West Bradford and Waddington;
for the renewal of churches who struggle to relate to their communities because of small congregations or lack of resources.

Holy and loving God,
in Jesus you walked the hills of Galilee
and the busy streets of Capernaum;
you addressed multitudes and had time for individuals.
Renew in us each morning the light of your presence,
that whatever the day brings
we may be channels of your renewing Spirit,
and share in your good purposes for the world,
in the name of Jesus Christ our Lord. Amen   *Robin Hutt*

Give thanks for the presence and power of the Holy Spirit

DAY 22

Make us, O blessed Master, strong in heart, full of courage and fearless of danger. Whatever lies before us upon our path, may we be strengthened by the might of your Spirit and delivered by your holy and gracious hand; and this we beg for your name's sake. Amen

F B Meyer, 1847-1929

Praying with Christians in the Far East

Japan

General Secretary of the Kyodan, the United Church of Christ in Japan:
Shiro Harada

Mission partners:
ed David and Keiko Gray, Elizabeth and Paul
ed Sheila Norris
sta+ Ian Smith

Give thanks for the witness of mission partners, a Christian presence in a largely secular nation, making a valuable contribution to its life through education.

Pray for the Kyodan as it reaches out to people who are searching for meaning;
for healing and unity where there are deep divisions among Christians;
for vision in the context of an ageing Church membership and the need to concentrate more on ministry and evangelism;
for continuing work through Bible classes that young Christians may grow in faith;
for Japan as a whole – for the influence of all who have a clear vision of a just and peaceful future, that Japan may become a valued part of the international community.

Korea

Presiding Bishop:
Kwang Young Chang

Mission partner:
th/ad Elinor Gordon°
(+CofS)
th+ Marlene Wilkinson°
(CMS)

Jesus, servant, at supper with your disciples,
you put a towel around your waist.
Like Peter, we protest
and distort your simple parable of love.
Wash us, Lord,
that we may be ready to wash each other's feet
and to serve one another for your sake.

Jesus, servant, unless your Spirit lives in us,
we will lord it over
the people and institutions in our care.
Come, dwell within us
and within our churches,
that we may learn how to follow you
who came not to be served but to serve
and to give your life as a ransom for many.

Prayer from Korea:
8th Assembly of the Christian Conference of Asia

Praying with Christians in Britain and Ireland

Give thanks for the work of District officers, circuit stewards and all who wrestle with politics and strategies for mission in ever-changing circumstances.
Pray for those who, though fully committed, are asked to do more, and those who are enthusiastic but tired by having much to do. May they be given strength to fulfil their calling and discernment to know what is most important;
for Methodist Homes, its headquarters staff in Derby and staff and residents of Queenswood in Nottingham.

Nottingham and Derby District

Chair:
Wesley Blakey
Secretary:
Averil George

An older woman's psalm
God, you have been my companion for so many years.
Out of my timidity you led me to open spaces,
you absorbed my anger and gave me back compassion,
you taught me to step out in trust however much I fear.

I am old now but as my body deteriorates,
memory fails and I may be winding down,
you have new lessons for me to learn,
new 'hills' to climb,
new ventures to undertake.

Asking for help I empower others,
accepting it I am a gift to the givers.
In my passivity my soul is growing strong.
Still you are my companion,
going ahead to be there when I cross over.
New every morning is your love.
>*Wanda Hayman, South West London*

In the freshness of a new-born child
   and the wrinkled face of age;
In hands which stretch out to be aided
   and the hands which clasp them;
In minds filled full of memory
   and heads excited with exploration;
We catch a glimpse of you.
We join our voices and our lives
   to the rising chorus of praise for your creation
   and limitless creativity.
>*Una McLean-Manning, Lincoln and Grimsby District*

Give thanks for the ministry of the Word, the sacraments and prayer

DAY 23

Draw near to your flock, O Shepherd of Israel, that we may rejoice at the sound of your voice; walk through the darkest shadows at your bidding and climb the rugged steeps under your protection. May we come at the last to the sight of your unclouded beauty where, in the glory of eternal light, you are worshipped for evermore. Amen   *Bede Jarrett, 1881-1934*

Praying with Christians in Australia and Aotearoa/New Zealand

Aotearoa/New Zealand

President:
David Bush

Eternal God, the same yesterday, today and for ever,
you are our secure reference point
in a constantly changing world.
Help us as we search for new ways to follow Christ,
ways that are relevant and meaningful for our time;
yet ways that are true to you
and to the rich heritage we have received from our past.
May your Spirit guide us in your love and grace,
that we may discover your future for us.
                    Bruce Anderson, minister of St John's, Levin

The Uniting Church of Australia (UCA)

President:
James Haire

Living Lord and Creator of all time,
our country celebrates 100 years as a new nation.
Help us, your Church, to live together in such a way
that demonstrates
   reconciliation between the original inhabitants
    and later arrivals,
   hospitality to those who come to us in hope and need,
    respect, care and openness
   towards those who hold strongly to different views
    about life and faith.
May the Uniting Church be a holy people,
a light to the nations, to your glory. Amen
                    Terence Corkin, General Secretary

Lord, we believe that you call us
to build a multi-cultural church together:
In which the uniqueness of each culture is not lost:
In which we can share and learn from each other...
Only with your Spirit will we be able to accomplish
   the task you have given us.   *Seongja Yoo-Crowe*
                    From the Mission Prayer Handbook of the UCA

Praying with Christians in Britain and Ireland

Give thanks for the Christian community at worship in village, town and city, witnessing in liturgy and life through preaching, prayer and presence to the truth of the gospel;
for our spiritual heritage reflected in worship, for perseverance in adversity, and for willingness to shape worship in new ways for unchurched generations.
Pray for Christians and churches touched by grace, able to communicate the good news to a world in pain;
for our new District Chair, developing her new pattern of ministry.

Oxford and Leicester District

Chair:
Alison Tomlin
Secretary:
Martin Wellings

Rural life
We pray for our fragile earth. Yesterday –
wild flowers, streams of clear water, busy farms.
Today – farmers bankrupt, streams polluted, flowers gone.
May we value creation, now, and be wise in its use.
God of creation, fertilise our minds.
We pray for the peace of the countryside. Yesterday –
quiet paths and byways.
Today – fast cars in narrow streets, crime in dark lanes.
May we recognise the good, now, despite the darkness.
God of light, clarify our vision.
We pray for a changing community. Yesterday –
its heart the church, the village shop.
Today – the shop closed, the church empty.
May we grow more aware of one another's needs.
God, all-embracing, infuse in us your caring.
We pray for a shrinking world. Yesterday –
divided by size and distance.
Today – Emails, the internet, telecommunication, satellite.
May we, in our insularity, be drawn closer to one another.
God of this one world,
bind us to our neighbour, everywhere. Amen

Alice Crosland, Buckingham

O God, as you have given yourself wholly for us
in our Lord Jesus Christ,
enable us to offer to you all that we are,
and all that your grace can make us.
In the name of Christ. Amen   *Martin Wellings*

Give thanks for our baptism and our call to serve Christ

DAY 24

Lord Jesus Christ, since you have taught us that we do not live by bread alone; feed us now and evermore with the true bread which comes down from heaven, even your own self, our Saviour and our Redeemer. Amen   *John Dowden, 1840-1910*

Praying with Christians in the Pacific (1)

Pacific Conference of Churches (PCC)

General Secretary:
Valamotu Palu

God, in your great mercy,
you raised Jesus Christ from the dead,
a source of living hope and power to all who struggle
to realise your peace and justice in the world.
Forgive us for seeking shelter behind the locked doors
of cultural divide and ethnic identities.
Breathe into us your Holy Spirit
and speak to us of your peace.
Come to us in your transforming power.
Burn the prejudice and hatred and fears in our lives.
Help us to receive the gospel of forgiveness into our lives
and to share in that same ministry of reconciliation,
within our own shores and in the whole world.
Amen   *Akuila Yabaki*

United Church in Papua New Guinea

Moderator:
Samson Lowa

Pray for the healing of memories for all the people of Bougainville;
for church leaders as they struggle with new issues in a changing society;
that the people of Papua New Guinea may be able to resist exploitation by unscrupulous operators competing for logging rights.

United Church of the Solomon Islands

Moderator:
Philemon Riti

Mission partners:
ad Roger and Connie Cann

Give thanks for the work of the Methodist Hospital (the oldest health care institution in the Solomon Islands) and for the work of Goldie College.
Pray for the continuing of the Peace Agreement;
for the Church and its leaders – for wisdom to deal with financial difficulties;
for Church leaders as they seek to find new ways to support their people in mission.
Forests are fast disappearing to make logging a major export: pray for wisdom in future developments;
for isolated rural communities and all who live close to the land.

Praying with Christians in Britain and Ireland

Give thanks for work with the homeless.
Please pray for those engaged in agriculture or fishing at a very difficult time, and those who minister to them; for those who care and witness in the city centre, in the inner city and on 'difficult' estates.

Plymouth and Exeter District

Chair:

Secretary:
Peter Williamson

Singing the Lord's song in a strange land
(Psalm 137.4)
Lord God, what a marvellous world you have created!
But sometimes I feel to be in a kind of 'Babylon':
Life is more like the Simpsons than the Waltons.
A strange land for the people of God.
Show us where we should be connected
And where we should be distinctive, Lord.
Make a difference in my life and let it show.
Let me recognise that the land is strange,
Even if I've lived here all my life.
Prevent me from being paralysed by these thoughts.
Help me make joyful connections,
To avoid ghetto-Christianity.
Give me such a passion to follow Jesus
That I can't help being different –
As Jesus was – loving sinners and rocking the boat.
Give me a passion for the Christ who died for me.
May I know the song of the gospel
And love you, Lord, with all I have.
Then may I sing the song
In the market places of the strange land
As well as in the safe, familiar corners of the church.
Phil Clarke, Director of Evangelism

Good Friday Walk of Witness

Not every morning, Lord, dawns like the first
    of school holidays
with a sense of freedom, excited by joy and adventure.
Some dawn, Lord, with the prospect of irksome duty,
    pain and weakness.
But in all you greet us with your fresh grace.
And, Lord, that is enough and more,
so we can live and live indeed.   *Kenneth Hext*

Give thanks for our part in the mission of Christ to the world

DAY 25

Grant, O God, that we who are one in our need of your forgiveness, may be one in our acts of compassion. May we who are made one in your love become one in our common life. May we who speak many languages dwell together as one race, in unity with our one heavenly Father; and this we ask through Christ our Lord. Amen

Queen Salote of Tonga, 1900-1965

Praying with Christians in the Pacific (2)

Tonga

Methodist President:
'Alifelete Mone

Give thanks for a strong commitment to Christian witness and the study of the Bible.
Pray for all who teach and lead young people that they may encourage them to hold on to traditional values;
for Taufa'ahau Tupou IV, King of Tonga.

Samoa

Methodist President:
Faáto'ese Auvaa

th/ed Roy° and Jo Newell

Give thanks for strong family and community ties.
Pray for continued commitment to mission locally and for Samoan Christians serving as mission partners in many parts of the world;
that the Church, in its concern about changing sea levels and increasing tropical storms, may be heard and make a difference to the decisions of world leaders;
for all who have left their homeland in search of work.

Fiji

Methodist President:
Tomasi Kanailagi

Pray for Ming-ya Tu'uholoaki (a National in Mission) who is doing pioneering work among the Chinese community;
for the Citizens Constitution Forum, a body set up to monitor human rights for all;
that true democracy will emerge.

Our God, the Lord of all creation,
we bring Fiji before you and its political turmoil,
the disunity and the suffering.
We pray that you will guide the leaders and their people
that they may seek everlasting peace in this country. Amen

Tomasi Kanailagi

Praying with Christians in Britain and Ireland

Give thanks for the discovery of new life and vitality arising out of District celebrations;
for a renewed sense of belonging to each other in the amalgamation of Cookstown and South Derry Mission circuits;
for the completion of building projects at Monaghan and Killylea, and for the blessing that Alpha continues to bring.
Pray for the new District Superintendent, Jim Rea, and other new ministers;
for the Charlemont and Cranagill circuit as they continue to work through the ramifications of stewardship;
for a new vision for the District;
for the ongoing situation at Drumcree.

Portadown District

Superintendent:
Jim Rea
Secretary:
Maurice Laverty

Pray for the Sheffield District Methodist Ministers' Housing Association, celebrating 50 years of providing houses for retired ministers;
for those in sector ministry, MLAs with other daytime jobs, those in college, prison, hospital and industrial chaplaincy and those who teach at the Urban Theology Unit and Cliff College;
for Cliff College as it embarks upon a £6.5 million development scheme.

Sheffield District

Chair:
David Halstead
Secretary:
Anne Brown

Every morning holds out the possibility of new beginnings,
 new dreams, new hopes, new ideas, new initiatives,
 new friendships, new encounters with Jesus,
 new experiences of God **for you.**
Every morning holds out the same possibility **for others**
 especially the people you will meet today.
Pray that what you do, say and are
 might make this a special day for them.
Pray that your smile, your love, your concern,
 your words, your silence,
 and the prayers you are saying now,
 might trigger a chain reaction
 which goes far beyond your immediate neighbourhood –
 encircling the world, and including the Sheffield District.
You can make a difference!
PS. Don't forget to pray for us and Portadown on Christmas Day!
David Halstead

Give thanks for unity, God's will and gift to the Church

Europe

'Christ calls us
out of our immobility
that we may be
uncomfortable.
But it is, at the same
   time,
a source of
encouragement...'

*Walter Klaiber,
Germany*

Republic of Ireland

In a post-conflict situation, traditionalist and triumphalist church thinking is being challenged to take risks in communicating the gospel and to attempt things that will fail unless God is at work in them.

Kenneth Todd

Al = Albania
Au = Austria
B = Belgium
Bo = Bosnia-Herzegovina
Cr = Croatia
Cz = Czech Republic
E = Estonia
G = Gibraltar
Gr = Greece
H = Hungary
L = Latvia
Li = Lithuania
Lu = Luxembourg
M = Moldavia
Mc = Macedonia
Mn = Montenegro
Sb = Serbia
Sl = Slovak Republic
Sn = Slovenia
Sw = Switzerland

Britain

British Methodist Districts

- dots are major towns and cities
- numbers correspond to the day in the Prayer Handbook

May the vitality
  of God's love
  refresh us;
may the depth
  of God's peace
  sustain us;
may the Spirit of God
  enfold us
each new day.

Ian White

DAY 26

The United Methodist Northern Europe Central Conference

Bishop:
Öystein Olsen

Superintendents:

Norway
Ola Westad, Arne Ellingsen

Sweden
Ulla Sköldh Jonsson, Anders Svensson, Håkan Englund, Ragne Fransson

Denmark
Ove Sörensen, Keld Munk

Finland
(Swedish language)
Gösta Söderström, Frederik Wegelius

Finland
(Finnish language)
Tapani Rajamaa

Estonia
Olav Pärnamets

Latvia
Arijs Viksna

Lithiuania
David Markey

Russia
Bishop of the UMC in Eurasia:
Rudiger Minor

Unite our hearts, O Lord, in bonds of affection that we may live with one another in humility and peace. Give us patience in the time of trial, and steadfastness in the tasks before us. Refresh our hearts in the hour of anguish and sustain us in the day of our need. Be to us, and to your whole Church, both our everlasting light and our eternal salvation; through Jesus Christ our Lord. Amen
Bernard Albert, 1569-1636

Praying with Christians in Europe

Give thanks for openness and intellectual honesty and missionary zeal;
for a sense of belonging to the wider, national and international community.
for a high regard for church tradition and ritual.
Pray for the Church, in former Communist countries, which is experiencing fatigue and economic difficulties after ten years of dramatic change and long-sought freedom;
for the new Tallinn United Methodist Church and mission centre, and for the reopening of the church in Vilnius;
for the new Theological Seminary starting correspondence courses in Estonian and Russian on the Internet;
for the growing indigenous leadership in **Lithuania**, including three candidates for the ministry.

Give thanks for a deepening spiritual fellowship in prayer, witness and service – 'that which binds us, despite all differences, is the love we have received and which is given freely to all the faithful' (Rudiger Minor);
for growth in the number of churches and members.
Pray for the active church in Ekaterinburg – its medical programme and prison ministry;
that more will respond to God's call to the pastoral ministry to care for churches that are understaffed.

The Conference of European Churches

General Secretary:
Keith Clements

Pray for the CEC member Churches as they discuss and implement the *Charta Ecumenica,* an important new ecumenical agreement presented to the Churches at Easter 2001.

Praying with Christians in Britain and Ireland

Southampton District

Chair:
Tom Stuckey
Secretary:
David Hinchcliffe

Give thanks for the many imaginative building schemes and for the provision, through the District Trustees, of financial help for mission, development and ministry;
for learning initiatives taken by local churches and circuits;
for the new opportunities of learning provided through the District 'Bread and Butter' programme with the URC, and for the work of our Training and Development Officer, Carol Gill;
for the work of Sarum College and the Southern Theological Education and Training Schemes and Networks.
Pray for an increased global vision and the development of new opportunities for friendship, learning, partnership and exchange through new links with the Methodist Church of Southern Africa;
for new ventures in evangelism and work with young people.

The day of grace
The long dark night is nearly over;
a hint of dawn is in the air.
The sleepless, who have spent a troubled night,
   wait for the morning.
The oppressed, who long for freedom,
   raise their eyes in hope.
The victims, who fear violence and abuse,
   greet the day with terror.
The mentally ill, their curtains drawn,
   both fear and long for light.
The fearful, who sit in darkness, cry out for peace.
For them and with them we pray,
   'Let this be the hour of redemption.'
'Let this be the day of grace.'
                      Tom Stuckey

Gracious God, giver of every new day,
we rejoice in your love for us
in every minute of our waking
and every moment of our sleeping.
May this new day find us following where you lead us
and serving where you call us. In Christ's name. Amen
              David Reddish, Bolton and Rochdale

Give thanks for the suffering and victory of Christ

DAY 27

May it please you, O Lord, to enlighten my heart with the fire of your love. I offer my hands to do your work, my lips to sing your praise and my life to proclaim your glory. Look upon my neighbours in their needs and guide me and bless me as I serve you in them; for Jesus' sake. Amen
Hildegard of Bingen, 1098-1179

Praying with Christians in Europe

The United Methodist German Central Conference

Bishop:
Walter Klaiber

Mission partners:
p John° and Lynda Atkinson
p Barry° and Gillian Sloan, Michael and Megan

Give thanks for signs of vitality amid decreasing membership and for the ordination of nine new pastors.
Pray with us that we may look critically at our way of being 'the church' in the light of the younger generation;
for wisdom and grace to deal with the growing racism and *Fremdenfeindlichkeit* (hostility to strangers). A German citizen of Mozambican origin died after being beaten up by three young men just because he was black. As we have a strong relationship with the Church in Mozambique, this made the incident even more shameful for us.
Pray for the growing number of African and international churches in our German UMC. *Thomas Kemper*

Pray for mission, 'to make known the love of God to people who are alien to church life, to invite them into the binding fellowship of our Church and to live with them a missionary life';
for ministry in East Germany amid rising unemployment which is causing promising young people to move away.

Belgium

President of the Eglise Protestante Unie:
Daniel Vanescote

We give thanks for the testimony of the Protestant congregations in ecumenical dialogue and for their common witness through centres of social service to cope with all sorts of urgent needs.
We pray for the future of the United Protestant Church in Belgium – for the growing together of Protestant and evangelical denominations. *Daniel Vanescote*

May Jesus Christ, the King of glory,
help us to make use of all the myrrh that God sends,
and to offer him the true incense of our hearts;
for his name's sake. Amen
Johannes Tauler, Germany, 1300-1361

Praying with Christians in Britain and Ireland

Give thanks for increasing numbers of circuits creatively wrestling with mission opportunities focusing money and people on locally chosen priorities.

Pray for churches of all denominations in the 'Inner Ring' of Bradford. May they be encouraged to work in new ways together through the ecumenical task group and its executive secretary Deacon Sue Brecknell.

May God grant to our District wisdom and insight in implementing our new and developing training policy to make us all more faithful disciples.

West Yorkshire District

Chair:
Peter Whittaker
Secretary:
Stuart Wild

Mission partners:
Alexander and Emily Siatwinda (Zambia)

Choices
Liberating God, you have endowed us as human beings with the freedom of choice.
Every day we live by our choices.

Today some people will be faced
with making very difficult choices –
painful choices in their relationships,
choices with unknown consequences
regarding their health or their future,
hard choices in their business connections
or at their place of work,
choices with long-term consequences for loved ones,
employees, patients or those convicted of crimes.

God of wisdom, we bring these people to you
that they may be given clarity
and sound judgement when utterly torn by their choices,
and strength and courage when a choice has to be made
but they are frightened by possible consequences.
And then may your peace be theirs. Amen
      Frank Hanson, Aotearoa/New Zealand

District celebration

May God who calls us
to follow in the way that is Jesus
equip us to fulfil our calling
in the power of the Spirit
serving the present age.   *Peter Whittaker*

Give thanks for the power of Christ to transform our suffering

DAY 28

United Methodist Central and Southern Europe Central Conference

Bishop:
Heinrich Bolleter

Superintendents:

Algeria

Austria
Helmut Nausner

Bulgaria
Bedros Altunian

Czech Republic
Josef Cervenak

Slovak Republic
Pavel Prochazka

Hungary
Istvan Csernak

Poland
Edward Puslecki

Switzerland/France
Urs Eschbach
Theo Rickenbacher
Hanna and Walter Wilhelm

Let your mighty hand and your outstretched arm, O Lord, be our defence. Let your mercy and loving-kindness in Christ Jesus be our protection. May your true and faithful Word be our instruction and guide; and may the grace of your life-giving Spirit be our comfort and strength, to the end and in the end, now and for ever. Amen *John Knox, 1513-1572*

Praying with Christians in Southern/Central Europe (1)

Pray for **Algeria** which has been engaged in a vicious and largely unreported civil war since 1992. Remember the quiet courage of Christians witnessing to a gospel of love in places where religion, ethnic identity and language have become reasons to rape, injure and kill;

for Methodists in **Switzerland** and **Austria** working together to produce a new Methodist Hymnal;
for ecumenical relationships in Austria, especially between Roman Catholic and Protestant Churches – for mutual support and the strengthening of each other's faith;

for Methodists in **Bulgaria** who have worked hard to build a good relationship with the State but fear the possibility of laws which may discriminate and restrict their freedom as a minority Church;

for mission in **Hungary** – for the new church centre in Budapest reaching out to the community;
for work with children and young people;
for congregations worshipping and seeking to carry out their mission with no facilities and poor church buildings.

Give thanks that the Methodist Church in **Poland** is beginning to be recognised and respected for its influence and outreach; that five new students (including, for the first time, two women – Joanna and Edyta) are being trained for the Methodist ministry; for the warm hospitality of Polish Christians;
for children's camps, especially one which brought together Polish and German children;

Pray for those for whom Auschwitz is more than a memory: that they may be encouraged to tell their story and find healing and peace;
that such atrocities may not happen again.

Praying with Christians in Britain and Ireland

Give thanks for the imaginative and courageous ways circuits and churches are developing new patterns of ministry and mission.
Pray for chaplaincies in industry and agriculture, hospitals and education, prisons and RAF bases across the District and for ministers serving in other and sector appointments.

A prayer for the adolescent
Father of all human beings,
we praise you for the innocence of childhood
and the joys and challenges of adolescence,
growing taller and developing
in an ever-expanding world of people and places,
and becoming co-ordinated in your presence.
Thank you for opportunities
to explore and recreate with our peers,
for friends who accept us,
teachers who equip us for the future,
for parents who love and understand us,
places to hang out,
the touch of a friend's hand,
and the discipline of arts and sports.
Loving God, be with all young people
and give them strength
to withstand the pressures that come their way.
Equip them in word and action
to be positive leaders in our society today.
Lord, as we think of your Son, Jesus Christ,
who was once a child like us,
we thank you for adolescence and youth. Amen
A young person, Bethel circuit, Barbados

Lord, take our tiredness of mind and body,
of spirit and understanding,
of living and commitment
and bring refreshment and new life
with the dew and sun of each new day.   *Peter Curry*

Wolverhampton and Shrewsbury District

Chair:
Peter Curry
Secretary:
Derrick Lander

Mission partners:
Solomona and Ana Potogi and Aristophane (Samoa)

Youth dance group

Give thanks for signs of renewal in the Church through the Holy Spirit

DAY 29

O most loving Shepherd, in the deepest of all waters we will trust you. In the darkest of all valleys we will rejoice in your presence. In the worst of our days we shall rest at peace in your arms. In the most troubled of our nights we shall be comforted by your saints. Amen

Archibald Campbell Tait, 1811-1882

Praying with Christians in Southern/Central Europe (2)

United Methodist Central and Southern Europe Central Conference (continued)

FR Yugoslavia

Superintendent:
Martin Hovan

Macedonia

Superintendent:
Wilhelm Nausner

We pray with all Christians in this region
for the long, slow process of healing
   the many different kinds of wounds and hurts;
for the setting up of a long-term strategy
   in conflict prevention;
for the building of peace and friendly co-existence;
for the building of bridges between religious traditions.
We pray that Serbs and Albanians may begin
   to live together in peace;
for an independent Kosovo,
   open to everyone who wants to work in harmony.
We pray for Methodist congregations who were scattered by the conflict and who are still refugees in other countries;
for a speedy humane solution for refugees, for their return in safety and dignity to their pre-war homes;
that churches in **Serbia** 'may be strengthened to witness to fundamental values of human dignity, justice and freedom and so assist a peaceful transition to a new democratic **Yugoslavia** under a government committed to human rights and in a society based on participation and dialogue';
that Church leaders may be given courage and strength to guide the Church in this process of change;
for the President of **Macedonia**, Mr Boris Trajkovski – a deeply committed Methodist Christian – for his leadership among the historic tensions between Slavs and Albanians; that Methodists may continue to play a significant role in humanitarian relief work and in democratic development.

Almighty God, from whom all thoughts of truth and peace proceed: kindle, we pray thee, in the hearts of all people the true love of peace, and guide with thy pure and peaceable wisdom those who take counsel for the nations of the earth; that in tranquillity thy Kingdom may go forward, till the earth is filled with the knowledge of thy love; through Jesus Christ our Lord. Amen

Francis Paget, 1851-1911

Praying with Christians in Britain and Ireland

We give thanks for the industrial chaplaincies in Hull, York and Selby;
for ecumenical partnerships and for the refurbishment of many properties.
We pray for all those affected by the floods over the past year, for families and friends involved in the Selby rail crash and for the farming communities.

York and Hull District

Chair:
Stuart Burgess
Secretary:
Rosemary Harrison

In suffering and loss
Lord of life, I'm angry, in shock and deep pain.
Why me? Why not someone else? Why those I love?
My lack of understanding frightens me.
At this moment it is hard to call you a loving Father.
In hope – desperation even – I cling
to the idea of a divine plan.
I begin to glimpse the suffering Jesus;
to discern your anguished face
as you watched him die, your Son;
to see the All-Powerful renouncing power.
Lord of life, I find it hard.
My head tries to explain what my heart doesn't feel.
Take my anger, frustration and gut-wrenching pain,
and turn them into something useful;
to bring comfort to others by being alongside them.
In the future, perhaps, but not yet, Lord.
All I want is to know that you're here with me;
that you understand all that I'm feeling,
and that you love me.
I don't need explanations right now;
I need to feel cuddled, safe, with you,
Lord of life and love.   *Michael King, World Church Office*

We give them back to thee, dear Lord,
who gavest them to us.
Yet as thou didst not lose them in giving,
so we have not lost them by their return.
For what is thine is ours always, if
we are thine.   *A Quaker prayer*

Give thanks for God's faithful departed servants who have revealed his grace and enriched our Christian pilgrimage

DAY 30

Grant to us, O Lord, that most excellent of all virtues, the gift of your divine love. Let love be in our thinking and our speaking, in our daily work and in the hidden places of our souls. Let love be in our friendships and in our life with those it is hard to bear. Let love be in our joys and in our sorrows, in our life and in our death. Amen *William Temple, 1881-1944*

Praying with Christians in Southern Europe

Portugal

Bishop:
Sifredo Teixeira

rt Cora Aspey

Give thanks for the development in **Portugal** of a ministry in folk and religious music and active evangelistic outreach; for the sharing of Christian literature with Churches in other Portuguese-speaking countries, especially Angola and Mozambique.

Pray for the Revd Délson Goulart Lessa, a mission partner from Brazil serving in **Portugal**;

Spain

President of Iglesia Evangelica Española:
Pastor Enrique Capo

for the work of the Seminario Unido Evangelico in Madrid, **Spain,** training ministers of several Protestant Churches; for the people of **Malta** as they seek solutions to the immense problems of pollution, increased waste, secularisation and the loss of traditional values which are the result of tourism; for the mission of the Church in this context.

Malta

p+ Colin Westmarland

Italy

Methodist President:
Valdo Benecchi

Mission partners:
p Richard°, Carol and John Grocott

O Lord our God,
thank you for the gift of prayer
that tears us away from our solitude;
for prayer that helps us to look
beyond the limits of our small Protestant minority;
for prayer that gives us strength to announce the gospel;
for prayer that goes beyond formal religious rites
and traditions, and which restores in us
a faith which is alive, and courageous in our service.
We pray that this year we may make our contribution
to ridding the world of violence in every form.
May we translate prayer into positive and concrete
commitment to service.
Help us to welcome with love
the many desperate people who enter our country
as they flee from war, poverty and slavery.
In the name of Jesus we pray. Amen *Valdo Benecchi, Italy*

Praying with Christians in Britain and Ireland

The Methodist Church in Scotland

Give thanks for the challenge to churches in Scotland to a deeper commitment to mission and unity as a result of the Scottish Church Initiative for Union;
for signs of renewal across the circuits;
for the success of Jubilee 2000 in Scotland, and for the setting up of Jubilee Scotland as its successor;
for the continued good work of NCH Scotland.
Pray for those affected by circuit boundary changes, that they may see new opportunities for mission and service;
for ministers and lay workers, often hard pressed to cope with demands made upon them in remote locations, by scattered membership and distance from worship centres;
for those committed to working with children and young people, especially in holiday clubs;
for the new Chair of the District.

Chair:
James Jones
Secretary:
David Cooper

Mission partners:
Charles° and Joyce Makonde (Kenya)

Shetland District

Give thanks for growing numbers of committed young people in our churches.
Pray for Deacon Elizabeth Colley, combining the role of District Training and Development Officer with ministry in six rural churches;
for the continuing ministry of the whole church in worship leading, children's and youth work and shared Christian witness across the islands.

Chair:
Richard Bielby
Secretary:
Malcolm McCall

Lord of the wild and rugged places,
Of wind and sky and ocean,
Be with us in the solitary moments of our lives.
Lord of the teeming urban streets,
Of office, shop and factory,
Be with us in the crowded moments of our lives.
Lord of all love, all joy, all peace,
Alongside us in suffering, grief and pain,
Help us to know you at the heart of our lives.   *Richard Bielby*

Working with children

© Rob Frost Team

Give thanks for our foretaste of the life of the world to come

Last day of the month

Lord, I bring the poverty of my soul to be transformed by your beauty; the wildness of my passions to be tamed by your love; the stubbornness of my will to be conformed by your commandments and the yearnings of my heart to be renewed by your grace; both now and for ever. Amen

Catherine of Genoa, 1447-1510

Praying with the World Council of Churches

2001-2010
Decade to Overcome Violence

We give thanks for the influence
of the World Council of Churches in social
and political affairs of many nations;
for all the encounters it facilitates across barriers of race,
culture and religious heritage.

Loving God, **forgive** the many times we have held back
and thought we had little to learn
from those whose experience is different from ours.
Make us more open to learn from the way of Christ
who made everyone feel welcome.

We pray for a stronger sense of community
through Churches Together in our local neighbourhood:
for the Week of Prayer for Christian Unity,
for the Good Friday Walk of Witness,
for ecumenical groups caring for people in need,
for churches known as Local Ecumenical Projects...
We pray for the **Churches Decade to Overcome Violence**

Scholarship students in countries other than Britain:

Juliana Braga (Brasil)

Amos Hounsa° (Benin)

Reuben Katana° (Kenya)

Kpoti Lassey° (Togo)

Roland Mae° (Solomon Islands)

Christian Nganji° (Cameroon)

Anil Reuben° (Fiji)

Janett Rojas (Peru)

Nathan° Samwini (Ghana)

that we may be able to challenge the spirit of violence
and affirm the way of reconciliation: to show,
by the healing of the wounds that have divided us,
that security grows out of co-operation and love.

With you is the fountain of life
God, our Father, give new courage to your pilgrim people. You bring forth life in the desert and water from the rock... May we and our churches support one another as we seek and thirst for you. Accompany us and show us your loving presence when the way is hard and we falter. Bring us to the unity you desire for your people, through Jesus Christ your Son and our Lord. Amen

Week of Prayer for Christian Unity 2002
© World Council of Churches

My computer

Dear God, please make my computer behave.
Let the battery charge and the orange light
   always be green.
Please make 'cut and paste' work when I am doing
   my dissertation,
And always make sure the floppy disk saves *everything!*

But most of all, dear Lord, I ask that I will not let
   the computer rule me.
You have provided alternatives (that are usually
   more reliable) for everything.
You created us to communicate with each other,
Not to sit endlessly at screens with aching eyes.

Please restrain me from spending loads of money
   on things that look useful but which I do not need.
Let me look at the real needs of the world, not at
   making profits for computer magnates.
My computer is useful but not essential,
So, if all fails on the computer front, let me praise
   your name (it will be a good thing in the long run).

Rachel Ullmer, USPG mission partner, Pakistan

Each day, someone, somewhere, asks:
Where is my God?
You wake up in the morning a blameless child, a mother;
your father dying of hunger, AIDS, or an incurable disease;
a neighbouring state goes to war,
innocent lives are lost, marriages break up,
women and children are abused, raped...
To whom do we run but you, O God?
In your Son, Jesus Christ, you have promised to save us.
Your salvation cannot be bought
   or destroyed by anything.
Prayerful lives draw us nearer to you.
Let every sunrise and sunset be with you, O God.
Through Jesus Christ your only Son our Saviour, we pray,
with thanksgiving in our hearts. Amen

*Richard Scott Luonde, at the United College of the Ascension,
from the Anglican Diocese of Northern Zambia*

Mission partners recently returned from overseas:

Andrew and Jill Baker (Grenada)
David Conkey (China)
Alan Cranmer (CSI)
Julie Crystal (China)
John and Anne Hogg (Zambia)
Michael and Sheila Holland (Nepal)
Tom Judd (Argentina)
Valerie King (China)
Rachel Nelson (CSI)
Alan Newton (Sri Lanka)
William Nightingale (Zambia)
Lisa Roberts (CSI)
Rebecca Robertson (Argentina)
Stephen° and Marlene Skuce (Sri Lanka)
Laura Smith (Fiji)
David° and Margaret° Stringer (Bolivia)
Jane Thompson (China)
Jason Waller (China)

Mission partners in transit or in training:

Vanessa Cook
Martin Stebbing
Ruth Watt
Elaine and John Woolley

Give thanks for the communion of saints

Lectionary of Readings, Hymns and Psalms 2001/2002

Readings broadly compare with the International Bible Reading Association's **Words for Today** (2001 and 2002). Explicit attention is given to various 'holy days' and other special occasions often celebrated. The **New Revised Standard Version** of the Bible has been used during preparation. Choice of psalms has been aided by the Methodist Sacramental Fellowship's **The Divine Office** (1975). The work has been undertaken by Philip Turner and Norman Wallwork.

Abbreviations: HP = **Hymns and Psalms** (1983) Ps = Psalm

Week beginning 2 September 2001: 22nd in Ordinary Time
Transformation

S	2	Jeremiah 2.4-13	HP713	Ps 81
M	3	Isaiah 51.1-16	HP711	Ps 119.17-32
T	4	Habakkuk 2.1-3	HP783	Ps 119.33-48
W	5	Isaiah 61.1-11	HP411	Ps 119.49-64
T	6	Isaiah 66.10-14	HP16	Ps 119.81-96
F	7	Ezekiel 47.1-12	HP402	Ps 119.97-112
S	8	Revelation 22.1-5	HP822	Ps 119.113-128

Week beginning 9 September: 23rd in Ordinary Time
Dreams coming True

S	9a	Jeremiah 18.1-11	HP404	Ps 139
M	10	Genesis 45.1-15	HP433	Ps 119.129-144
T	11	Deuteronomy 30.15-20	HP684	Ps 1
W	12	Matthew 11.2-6	HP744	Ps 119.145-176
T	13	Acts 2.1-18	HP486	Ps 136
F	14b	John 3.13-17	HP179	Ps 22
S	15	Philemon	HP757	Ps 140

[a = Racial Justice Sunday; b = Holy Cross Day]

Week beginning 16 September: 24th in Ordinary Time
Beyond our Dreams

S	16	Jeremiah 4.11-28	HP712	Ps 14
M	17	1 Kings 3.1-15	HP674	Ps 138
T	18	Ezekiel 1.22-28	HP8	Ps 2
W	19	Isaiah 60.1-22	HP125	Ps 3
T	20	Luke 15.1-10	HP69	Ps 5
F	21c	Matthew 9.9-13	HP706	Ps 119.65-80
S	22	Acts 26.4-23	HP693	Ps 9

[c = Matthew, Apostle and Evangelist]

Week beginning 23 September: 25th in Ordinary Time
Times for Change

S	23	Jeremiah 8.18 - 9.1	HP39	Ps 79
M	24	Amos 6.4-7	HP347	Ps 146
T	25	Isaiah 14.8-17	HP676	Ps 11
W	26	Jeremiah 6.9-15	HP408	Ps 16
T	27	Jeremiah 23.1-4	HP772	Ps 23
F	28	Luke 16.14-18	HP409	Ps 27
S	29d	Revelation 12.7-12	HP20	Ps 103

[d = Michael and All Angels]

Week beginning 30 September: 26th in Ordinary Time
Necessity for Change

S	30	Jeremiah 32.1-15	HP672ii	Ps 91
M	1	Amos 8.4-7	HP439	Ps 113
T	2	Luke 16.19-31	HP804	Ps 30
W	3	James 5.1-6	HP406	Ps 31
T	4	Hebrews 5.1-10	HP235	Ps 32
F	5	Luke 18.1-8	HP215	Ps 34
S	6	Isaiah 65.17-25	HP769	Ps 36

Week beginning 7 October: 27th in Ordinary Time
Possibility for Change

S	7	Lamentations 3.19-26	HP252	Ps 137
M	8	1 Samuel 2.1-10	HP86	Ps 38.1-9
T	9	Luke 18.18-30	HP767	Ps 38.10-22
W	10	Luke 19.1-10	HP220	Ps 39
T	11	Luke 19.45-48	HP485	Ps 40
F	12	Luke 20.1-8	HP219	Ps 41
S	13	James 1.9-18	HP707	Ps 44

Week beginning 14 October: 28th in Ordinary Time
Praying for Change

S	14	Jeremiah 29.1-7	HP510	Ps 66
M	15	Luke 11.1-4	HP134	Ps 49
T	16	Luke 11.5-13	HP719ii	Ps 50
W	17	Luke 18.9-14	HP701	Ps 51
T	18e	2 Timothy 4.5-17	HP710	Ps 147
F	19	1 Kings 8.33-43	HP558	Ps 53
S	20	1 Timothy 2.1-8	HP411	Ps 54

[Week of Prayer for World Peace; e = Luke the Evangelist]

Week beginning 21 October: 29th in Ordinary Time
Respect for Change

S	21	Jeremiah 31.27-34	HP783	Ps 119.97-104
M	22	Ruth 1.1-14	HP68	Ps 104.1-23
T	23	Ruth 1.15-22	HP33	Ps 104.24-35
W	24	Ruth 2.1-23	HP754	Ps 147
T	25	Ruth 3.1-18	HP748	Ps 148
F	26	Ruth 4.1-12	HP370	Ps 149
S	27	Ruth 4.13-22	HP85	Ps 150

[One World Week]